His
Name
Is
Joel

His Name Is Joel

Searching for God in a Son's Disability

Kathleen Deyer Bolduc

Bridge Resources
Louisville, Kentucky

Unless otherwise noted, Scripture quotations are from the New Revised Standard Version of the Bible, copyright © 1989 by the Division of Christian Education of the National Council of the Churches of Christ in the U.S.A. Used by permission. Scripture quotations may have been edited for inclusivity.

Every effort has been made to trace copyrights on the materials included in this book. If any copyrighted material has nevertheless been included without permission and due acknowledgment, proper credit will be inserted in future printings after notice has been received.

This resource was made possible by funds given for the Operation Dignity project of the Bicentennial Fund. Grateful acknowledgment is made for those gifts.

Edited by Cassandra D. Williams

Book and cover design by Claire Calhoun

First edition

Published by Bridge Resources
Louisville, Kentucky

Web site address: http://www.bridgeresources.org

PRINTED IN THE UNITED STATES OF AMERICA

99 00 01 02 03 04 05 06 07 08 — 10 9 8 7 6 5 4 3 2 1

Library of Congress Cataloging-in-Publication Data

Bolduc, Kathleen Deyer, date.
   His name is Joel : searching for God in a son's disability /
Kathleen Deyer Bolduc. — 1st ed.
     p. cm.
   Includes bibliographical references.
   ISBN 1-57895-034-1
   1. Bolduc, Kathleen Deyer, date. 2. Bolduc, Joel Christopher. 3. Parents of handicapped children—Biography. 4. Parents of handicapped children—Psychology. 5. Parents of handicapped children—Religious life. 6. Mentally handicapped children—Family relationships. 7. Parent and child—Religious aspects—Christianity. I. Title.
HQ759.913.B65 1999
649'.151'092—dc21   99-25594

Contents

Acknowledgments   vii

Introduction   ix

Perfect Love   1

In My Distress I Call Upon the Lord   4

Simple Choices   6

Breath of Life   10

A Heritage from the Lord   12

Fear and Foreboding   15

A Vote of Confidence   18

Taking the Plunge   21

His Name Is Joel   25

Difficult Choices   27

High-Wire Artist   31

When the Righteous Cry for Help   35

Garments of Praise   40

Light Rising in Darkness   42

Deceived and Abandoned   45

I Lie Awake   48

Deceived by Pride   50

From the Precipice   54

Be Angry, but Do Not Sin   58

Forgiveness   61

Your Child Is Not Welcome Here   64

Abundant Comfort   68

The Refiner's Fire   72

Victory in Tribulation   75

Guilt—The Enemy   79

Talk to Me!   82

And a Little Child Shall Lead Them   86

Running Strong   89

The Essence of Joel   93

The Gift of Friendship   96

I Will Give You Rest   99

Time Away   102

Rivers in the Desert   105

Simple Gestures   108

Joy Rekindled   111

The Maestro   113

I'm Naked and I'm Dancing!   116

The Sacred Place   119

Epilogue   123

Acknowledgments

The birth of this book would not have been possible without the love and support of the following people and organizations.

Thank you, Wally, Matt, Justin, and Joel for allowing me to fling open the doors and windows of our private lives. I pray that the winds of the Spirit may blow through and bless others whose homes have been touched by disability. Wally, for your joyful presence in my life I am ever grateful. Thank you for sharing both laughter and tears along the journey.

I owe the Earlham School of Religion, Richmond, Indiana, a debt of gratitude for its generosity in awarding me the Patrick Henry Writing Scholarship and for allowing me the luxury of working on this manuscript, undisturbed, in Elton Trueblood's Teague Library. I am especially grateful for Tom Mullen's guidance and encouragement. Thank you, Tom, for believing in me as a writer when I didn't believe in myself.

For nourishing the seed of this book with optimum growth conditions in the form of excellent teaching, critiques, fellowship, and prayer support, I have The Writing Academy to thank. A heartfelt thanks to my instructors in that organization, especially Evelyn Minshull for her help with this manuscript. Hugs to Patty Kyrlach who never doubted that this book would see print.

My graduate work at The College of Mount Saint Joseph in Cincinnati, Ohio, concentrated in the area of disability's effect on the family system, was instrumental in confirming the universality of the grief process experienced by parents of children with disabilities. Thank you for giving me the courage to reach out to others with this story.

I am richly blessed with family and friends whose support and prayers sustain me. I thank each and every one of you for loving and accepting me just as I am.

I count myself most fortunate to have been able to work with my editor, Cassandra Williams, on this project. Thank you,

Casey, for your graciousness, your enthusiastic support, your heart for ministry, and for believing in the worth of this work.

Joel, the greatest gift you have given me is the gift of your unpretentious, unadorned, spontaneous self. Thank you so much for being who you are, for opening my spirit to the deeper truth of what it means to be human, and for teaching me so much about the kingdom of God here on earth. You truly are my pearl beyond price. I dedicate this book to you.

Introduction

Journeying through the wasteland of grief is lonely. I know. I've traveled this land for thirteen years since the birth of my third son, Joel Christopher. Joel has moderate mental retardation and mild autism.

This is the story of my search for God in the midst of disability; the story of my attempt to make sense of something utterly senseless—a beautiful boy with a damaged brain.

After a difficult birth and a bout of severe jaundice, it became obvious within the first few months of his life that something was not right with Joel's development. A combination of inaccurate diagnosis and deep denial kept me and my husband Wally from accepting the severity of Joel's condition for many years. Denial kept us from drowning in a truth we were not yet ready to face. Finally, as Joel approached kindergarten age, emotionally bruised and battered by a reality we could no longer deny, we sought a multifactored evaluation. The diagnosis: moderate mental retardation, a diagnosis which accounted for developmental timetables not yet met. It took another five years, however, to diagnose Joel's unexplainable and hard-to-live-with behaviors as autistic tendencies.

Accepting a child's disability involves the death of a dream. All parents dream as they wait for a child to be born; dreams as numerous and unique as the parents-to-be that dream them: teddy-bear tea parties; Saturday morning soccer games; hand-made Halloween costumes; stock car races; piano lessons, or perhaps Suzuki violin; cross-country camping; trophy shelves flanking the fireplace.

When Joel was ten, I went back to school to pursue a master's degree in religious and pastoral family studies. Concentrating on the effects of a child's disability on the family system, I learned that dealing with a death, even the death of a dream, involves maneuvering one's way through the stages of grief: denial, anger, bargaining, depression, and acceptance. The stages come and go, sometimes in this sequence, sometimes not. The dreamed-of child will never be. Nothing is certain except for this: Priorities will change, goals will shift, life will take a new trajectory.

In all the uncertainty and confusion of grieving for the lost dream, one truth is unavoidable. Until a parent faces the pain of loss and brokenness, he or she cannot begin the journey toward healing, wholeness, and acceptance.

As I struggled to come to terms with Joel's disability, in those ten long years before learning that this grief experience is universal, how I longed for a map of the journey! For footprints to follow through foreign territory. Too proud and isolated by pain to ask for help, I made several searches of the library and bookstores, hoping to find a book, written by another parent in a similar circumstance, that would make sense of my inner struggle. When the search proved fruitless, I had no choice but to go directly to the ultimate Map-Maker; the source of all knowledge, all meaning, all direction in life.

I carried my anger, my despair, and my need for meaning to God.

This book is the result. It is an eyewitness account of God's presence in a little boy with a damaged brain.

I offer these footprints of a mother's journey through grief toward a place called acceptance with the prayer that they may hasten healing and hope in the lives of others who struggle to find God in a child's disability. For those who love, work, and worship with such parents, may it give birth to deeper understanding and compassion. And for those readers who journeyed alongside me through the years of my denial and anger, I pray these words will not be read as a reproach. I had then no words to explain my struggle, to reach out and ask for help. Finally, the words have come. May they go out only as a blessing.

Perfect
Love

God is love, and those who abide in love abide in God, and God abides in them. . . . There is no fear in love, but perfect love casts out fear.

—1 John 4:16, 18

February 27, 1985. Standing sideways I held up the hospital gown, presenting the silhouette of my swollen belly to the camera. Wally fiddled with the focus and clicked a picture. "For posterity," he said with a laugh.

Looking down, I wondered at the awesome miracle of conception and birth. Who was this person we had created, who ballooned my belly to such great proportions? Boy or girl? Strong-willed or docile? Introvert or extrovert? Pulling the gown down, I climbed back into the birthing bed and shivered in anticipation.

The labor progressed with ease. This was my third pregnancy, and Wally had successfully coached me through the last two deliveries without medication. Saving energy for the big moment, he snoozed in a chair beside the bed. I concentrated on breathing, letting waves of contractions work unhindered. The nurse was impressed.

Then came the irresistible urge to bear down. "Not yet," the nurse cautioned. "Let me get the doctor."

She scooted out of the room. Wally sat up, rubbing his eyes.

"I can't keep from pushing," I panted. Panic welled up. Wally laid a cool hand on my forehead. "You're all right. You can do it. Relax."

"Okay. Go ahead and push." The doctor's deep voice, immediately curbing fear, sounded from the foot of the bed. Eyes closed, face contorted, I pushed with every muscle in my body.

"We've got a problem here. I'm going to do an episiotomy. Let's get this baby out quickly." I opened my eyes and saw the doctor's grim face at the foot of the bed. I clamped them shut again.

Wally's disembodied voice floated from behind my head.

"What's happening? What are all these people doing in here?" I sensed panic behind his words. In my concentration, I couldn't pry my eyes open. Who was he talking about?

"Just a little problem. We'll get it under control. One more good push now and we'll have it."

I pushed, felt I would split apart, then felt sudden relief. Opening my eyes, I watched the baby's head emerge from my body. Miracle of miracles. I also saw three strange people standing around the bed. Tentacles of fear clutched at my heart, only to be borne away on waves of an intense contraction.

"A boy!" the doctor shouted a few moments later. He held up our son. Wrinkled, red, and utterly beautiful. Joy, as effervescent as champagne, bubbled through my consciousness. Wally leaned down and kissed my head. The doctor handed the baby to the masked strangers, who whisked him off to a corner of the room.

"What's going on?" Wally asked as his hand squeezed mine.

"Everything's fine," the doctor replied. "Your wife still has some work to do. Let's concentrate on finishing up, OK? You'll be able to hold him in a minute or two."

His words reassured me.

Liquid love coursed through my veins.

Bursting with joy at our achievement, I uttered a silent prayer of thanksgiving.

Dear Lord, what a miracle! Intense pain replaced so quickly with over-whelming joy! Nine long months of suspense, culminating in the words, "It's a boy!" This child, so long in the dark, suddenly wrapped in the light of a whole new world. The child I've waited so long to hold, nuzzled safe and warm against my breast. Thank you for these treasured moments. Moments of awe and wonder as we marvel at the perfection of our newborn son, Joel Christopher. Moments free from fear. Moments of perfect love, carved into our hearts. Amen.

In My Distress I Call Upon the Lord

In my distress I called
upon the LORD;
  to my God I cried
  for help.
From God's temple God
heard my voice,
  and my cry to God
  reached God's ears.

—Ps. 18:6

"He's orange," my sister-in-law squawked. My newborn son lay pumpkin-faced in his crib. Her comment confirmed what I'd already suspected. Jaundice. I made a quick phone call and bundled Joel into his snowsuit for a trip to the doctor's office.

The head nurse met us at the reception desk, took one look and said, "Don't bother to take off the snowsuit. Take him down to Children's Hospital. He looks pretty bad."

My throat swelled. The hospital? This was supposed to be a quick, routine visit. My firstborn had also developed jaundice. No big deal.

Heart pounding in my ears, I buckled Joel into his car seat. Even in the bulky blue snowsuit he looked small and defenseless. Had it been only a week before I had marveled at his hugeness? I remembered the doctor turning from the delivery room scales and announcing, "Ten pounds. How about that?"

Under the fluorescent lights of the hospital waiting room, Joel's skin glowed orange. I held him tightly against my chest and kissed his head. The green plastic chairs were all occupied by other parents waiting with their children. Most of them sat and read, babies sleeping in infant carriers on the floor or on the chairs next to them.

Why aren't you holding your baby? I wanted to scream at the woman next to me. *Don't you know she needs to be held? You're wasting precious time with that book. Pick up your baby!* My eyes stung and my head throbbed with the injustice of it. Obsessed by the complacency around me, I wrapped my arms more tightly around Joel. It was sinful, the way they sat there, indifferent to their babies. The man sitting across from me watched a noisy game show on TV, ignoring the coos and gurgles coming from the baby at his feet. *Your child is a miracle! A gift from God! Pick him up and hold him!*

The words formed in my mind, unspoken. My prayers rose up, unbidden. I kissed away the tears that fell on Joel's head. The salty taste on my tongue was the taste of fear.

Lord, do you hear my voice from your temple? Do my cries really reach your ears? Help me believe your Word. So often when fear consumes me, I forget you are there, waiting with comforting arms. Surround me with those loving arms, Lord, and banish the fear that holds me captive. Amen.

Simple Choices

Give ear to my
prayer, O God;
   do not hide yourself
   from my supplication.
Attend to me, and
answer me;
   I am troubled
   in my complaint.
I am distraught.
                    —Ps. 55:1–2

"It's really a very simple choice, Mrs. Bolduc," the doctor said in a crisp, impersonal voice. "You can leave the baby there at the hospital, where they'll put him under the bilirubin lights, or you can take him home. If you choose to take him home, you'll have to bring him in daily for blood tests so we can monitor the bilirubin count. No breast-feeding until we get the jaundice under control."

"Why is that?" My voice wavered.

"This type of jaundice is often exacerbated by breast milk." The phone line crackled with his impatience. I wondered how many patients, willing to pay $30.00 a visit, were waiting outside his door. Why did *my* pediatrician have to be out of town now, of all times?

"But he's only a week old," I wailed. "How important is it to put him under the lights? I don't want to leave him here alone! He needs me!"

"Mrs. Bolduc, as I said, it's totally up to you. Start him on formula tonight, bring him in every day for testing, and the bilirubin count should start falling within a few days. Let the doctor there at the hospital know your decision." The dial tone hummed in my ear.

Slamming the receiver down, I choked back tears and looked around for my mother who had driven us to the hospital. I didn't see her. What should I do? What should I do? What should I do? The words galloped through my mind in a Dr. Seuss-like rhythm. I picked up the phone and dialed Wally's office. "You have reached the office of Modern Material Handling. No one is in the office right now . . ." The receiver dangled from my hand as I stared at the floor. The patterns in the linoleum changed shape through the prism of unshed tears. Already at the point of exhaustion from the birth just a few days before, I felt dazed and unsure of myself. Mom appeared around the corner, carrying Joel. Seeing my distress she hugged me with her free arm, but what I wanted was someone to make the decision for me. That, she couldn't do.

I took my baby home.

On the way home from the hospital, we stopped at a medical supply store where I rented a breast pump. It was important to keep up my milk supply. I couldn't imagine bottle-feeding for a few days, much less throughout Joel's infancy. I had nursed both Matt and Justin through their first year, and the warmth of those precious bodies against my chest, skin-to-skin, had sustained my soul as much as my milk sustained their bodies. The thought of a hard, sterile bottle separating me from this baby, especially when we were just starting to get to know each other, undammed the tears. I cried the rest of the way home.

"I'm scared," I whispered to Wally in bed that night. "Really scared."

"Everything's fine," he said in a loud, firm voice, as if the volume and weight of the words proved them more true. "The doctor gave you a choice, right? He wouldn't have done that if both options weren't advisable. Quit worrying." He reached over and gave me a sleepy kiss before settling into his pillow. A few moments later, he was snoring.

Unable to heed his advice, I spent the next week worrying—worrying while I sterilized bottles, worrying while I tried to force the unfamiliar bottle nipple into Joel's mouth, worrying while I fought to get him to drink enough formula, worrying while I pumped my breasts in the privacy of our bedroom. Adding to the stress, pumping extra milk was difficult and time-consuming. I felt like a dairy cow, and wouldn't even allow Wally into the room while using the pump.

Meanwhile, we made the trek to Children's Hospital daily. Every day, the nurses pricked Joel's little foot for blood. It took me ten to fifteen minutes to calm him after the blood test. We waited daily for the results. For the first several days, the bilirubin count rose and then held steady in the midteens. Every day, worry grew within me, ugly and unwanted.

Finally, on the fourth day a talkative nurse made a comment that knotted my stomach. "They almost always hospitalize babies when the count is this high."

I immediately called the pediatrician's office. My doctor was still on vacation, and I found myself talking to the same doctor who had given me the choice of daily blood tests or hospitalization. When I confronted him with what the nurse had said, he responded angrily.

"I'm the physician here, Mrs. Bolduc. We will give it one more day. If the bilirubin count is still high tomorrow, we will talk about our options. Good-bye." So much for bedside manners.

The next day the count began falling. Two days later, it had returned to normal, and I was able to begin nursing again. The intimacy of cradling my newborn next to my breast during feeding time helped relieve much of the stress. Yet a very quiet, amorphous fear hid itself well in the back of my mind. I didn't mention it to Wally. I knew what his response would be.

"Everything will be just fine, Kate. Everything will be just fine."

Dear Lord, take away this unnamed fear. Like an enemy trained in guerrilla warfare it preys on my subconscious, hiding itself when I try to confront it. I want to believe, as Wally does, that everything will be just fine. Oh Lord, I want to believe. Help me believe. Amen.

Breath
of Life

Then the LORD God formed man from the dust of the ground, and breathed into his nostrils the breath of life; and the man became a living being.

—Gen. 2:7

We lay snuggled together, my baby Joel and I. I on my side, he on his stomach, head nestled in the crook of my arm. I breathed gently, quietly, on his sweet-smelling head. With the rhythm of my breathing came a prayer. "Spirit of God, Spirit of God, Spirit of God."

My breath, the source of my aliveness, surrounded my son with warmth, and peace, and love. He stirred, yawned, and settled back into sleep with a contented sigh. I continued surrounding him with my breath, my being, my love.

I marveled at the way my child was teaching me about the love of God. When God created Adam out of the dust of the earth he "breathed into his nostrils the breath of life." One of the Hebrew words for breath is *nephesh,* life-giving breath, Spirit of God. Spirit of God residing within us.

Praying for the Spirit, I was filled to overflowing. We lay snuggled together, my baby Joel and I, warm breath and prayer surrounding my child with life-sustaining love. And while we rested, the Holy Spirit, God's breath of life, surrounded us both with love-sustaining life.

Lord, I come before you with a joyful and thankful heart. I thank you for the breath of life you give to each one of us on our physical birth. And for your Holy Spirit, Lord, breathed into us as a gift when we but ask. As for the gift of my child, Lord, I bow before you in thanksgiving. Amen.

A Heritage from the Lord

Like arrows in the
hand of a warrior
  are the sons of
  one's youth.
Happy is the man
who has
  his quiver full of them.

—Ps. 127:4–5

Three sons! What a blessing! Matt and Justin, ages eight and five, greeted their baby brother with enthusiastic hugs and kisses ("I sure am glad you had a boy, Mom. We didn't want any dumb girls around here!"). Justin enjoyed playing with the baby ("How do I make him smile, Mom?"), and Matt acted matter-of-fact about the family's new addition ("He doesn't do much, does he?"). We settled into a routine, and it was soon hard to remember life without baby Joel. Matt and Justin left for school every morning, returning by late afternoon, leaving me plenty of time for Joel, to catch a catnap, or to keep up with the housework. Life was good.

And then came summer vacation. Matt and Justin were little tornadoes blowing through the house and out again, leaving a path of destruction in their wake. They wrestled, scattered toys, threw shoes and socks around with abandon, emptied the refrigerator, and made noise. Lots of noise. They argued, yelled, slammed doors, and asked endless questions. I suddenly found myself exhausted and grumpy instead of energized and full of praise, short-tempered and frustrated rather than patient and thankful. I craved the impossible—peace.

One afternoon Justin dashed in the door and skidded to a stop in front of the couch where I sat nursing the baby. He stood there for a moment, transfixed by the sight of his little brother at my breast. Joel turned his head just far enough to see Justin, waved his arms in a wriggly greeting, and continued to suck. Justin plopped down next to me, worming his way under my free arm.

"What do you say we spend some time together tonight, Mommy?" Blue eyes gleamed bright in his narrow, freckled face. This was serious, five-year-old business!

"What do you have in mind?"

"Oh, I don't know. Maybe ice cream at the Creamy Whip?" He reached over and tickled Joel under the chin. Joel stopped eating long enough to grin.

"Sounds good to me," I answered sleepily.

I had to be reminded after dinner. While eating I'd been entertaining thoughts of climbing into bed and finishing the novel I'd begun the day before. Getting into the car and going for ice cream wasn't a high priority. But I'd promised.

I left Wally at home in charge of Matt and Joel, and half an hour later Justin and I lay in the middle of the grassy commons across the street from the Creamy Whip. Justin had insisted we bring a blanket. Sticky and satisfied after our ice cream, we lay back to watch the towering thunderheads filling the twilight sky. Neither of us said a word for some time, and the silence between us resounded with pleasant thoughts and the noises of the community; cars driving past, lawn mowers buzzing, barking dogs, and children calling to one another in play. The clouds piled higher, and the setting sun tinged their edges with gilt.

Justin broke my reverie. "I love you, Mom." He reached over and grabbed my hand.

"Why, thanks, sweetie. I love you too. I'm glad you had this idea." (And I had wanted to hide in my room with a book!)

"You know what?" He paused, looking up at the sky. "I decided you're the prettiest Mom I know. Prettier than Aaron's, or Bill's, or John's . . . prettier than any of 'em!" He stared at me intently.

"Gee, thanks, Jus! What a compliment!" I certainly hadn't been feeling pretty lately—fifteen pounds overweight, a new baby, two active boys, a complaining spirit. It was quite a compliment, indeed. I felt the sleeve of care, so tightly knit over the course of the summer, relax and fall away. Reaching over, I ruffled Justin's sun-bleached hair.

My complaining spirit exploded into a hymn of praise. All because of a five-year-old's wish for time alone with Mom, an ice cream cone, and a blanket in the grass on a summer evening. Alleluia! Alleluia!

Dear Lord, the psalmist was right. These sons are a heritage from you, indeed. Let me never take their preciousness for granted. Create within me a thankful spirit, even on days when the noise and commotion seem too much. Amen.

Fear and Foreboding

Your eyes beheld my unformed substance. In your book were written all the days that were formed for me, when none of them as yet existed.

—Ps. 139:16

Vacationing in Michigan in June 1985, we called Wally's cousins, who lived in the area, and invited them to the lake for a cookout. After a meal of hot dogs and hamburgers, the guys gathered on lawn chairs facing the lake, the older children played tag, and the women gathered inside to escape the noise and mosquitoes.

By coincidence, three of us had four-month-old babies. We exchanged war stories of the births, passed the babies around with oohs and aahs, commented on family likenesses, and talked about the developmental milestones already passed in their short lifetimes.

An uneasy feeling grew in the pit of my stomach. Bonnie's baby looked so wiry and strong. Lying on the floor, she craned her neck to catch all the action in the room. She rolled over several times and waved her arms wildly when anyone looked her way.

Linda's little one, a bruiser named Jonathan, looked like the Gerber baby. He, too, held up his head with ease. Pumping his fat legs in the air, he blew bubbles and chortled happily. Everyone laughed at his antics.

Joel, on the other hand, lay with great calm in the middle of his blanket. Lifting his head, he would look around the room quickly, and then down his head flopped, as though too heavy for his neck to support. While bright-eyed like the other babies, Joel felt like a rag doll in my arms.

Once we'd made it through the jaundice scare, and once Joel started gaining weight (his first month's checkup showed he'd lost weight), I was convinced I had been blessed with the world's perfect baby. Unbelievably calm and placid, Joel was a gift. Our first two sons had been born in the midst of my father's illness, and both pregnancies had been filled with worry and sadness.

My father died when I was seven months pregnant with our second son, and Justin's nature reflected the emotional strain I'd been under. Extremely active, he cried often to vent energy, refused cuddling and rocking, and crawled and walked months ahead of schedule.

Unlike the other two, my third pregnancy had been free of turmoil. Joel was a snuggler from the start. I rocked him for hours at a time, drinking in his baby scent, coaxing those first smiles, reveling in his beauty. He rarely cried, slept through the night within a month of birth, and napped both morning and afternoon. With Matt and Justin both in school, I seized the time, let the housework wait, and enjoyed my baby.

The beginning of the week at the cabin had been perfect, even though the skies were overcast and the temperature cool. Not to be stopped, Wally, Matt, and Justin bundled up every morning and hiked the trails around the lake, fished from the pier, and rowed a gray and misty lake. Appreciating the peace and quiet, I stayed at the cabin with Joel. Armed with a stack of books, I curled up next to the fire and read for hours at a stretch, praising God for the blessing of such a serene baby.

Now, sitting among a group of relatives, a seed of doubt sprouted upward. As in time-lapse photography, the uneasiness sown during the birth and jaundice episode broke the soil of my consciousness, quickly stretched forth its stem, and unfurled its head into a feeling of raw fear.

What I had viewed as a blessing—Joel's sleeping through the night, long naps, his peaceful nature—now seemed sinister. Foreboding filled my spirit as I sat nursing my son in a Michigan cabin, surrounded by the sounds of women laughing and babies gurgling.

Something was wrong with my baby.

Lord, your Word tells me you hold Joel's life in your hands. That you, in your omniscience, know what lies ahead of him in the years to come. My heart tells me I should trust you and the plan you have for my son. Why, then, this sick feeling in the pit of my stomach? Fear and foreboding have taken up residence in my spirit. Reassure me, Lord. Reassure me. Amen.

A Vote of Confidence

I t is better to take refuge in the LORD
than to put confidence in mortals.
It is better to take refuge in the LORD
than to put confidence in princes.

—Ps. 118:8–9

My vacation realization that Joel wasn't developing properly sent me directly to the pediatrician on our return home.

"Why is Joel so floppy?"

"Why isn't he rolling over yet?"

Month after month, I pestered him with questions.

"Is there something wrong with his muscles?"

"Shouldn't he be sitting up by now?"

"What's wrong with my baby?"

Every question elicited the same response.

"Some babies are floppier than others, Mrs. Bolduc. I don't think there's anything to worry about yet. Let's wait and see."

In the meantime, comparing Joel with other babies became an

obsession. Although he was cuter and more sociable than many, he never measured up developmentally.

"Quit comparing," the doctor said. "All babies develop at their own rate; you know that." He riffled through our family's records as we talked. "It says here that Matt walked at fourteen months, and Justin at nine. That's quite a difference! We'll consult a specialist if necessary, but for now I say wait and see."

I had great respect for this doctor. He treated everyone with consideration, didn't rush patients through the office, answered questions thoroughly, and never complained about middle-of-the-night phone calls. Best of all, the kids loved him. Doctors who wear Mickey Mouse ties and tickle bellies are hard to come by.

We waited.

Joel, meanwhile, charmed his big brothers, the teens in our youth group, the extended family, an entire neighborhood, and strangers on the street. The attraction lay in an eye-crinkling grin, dimples creasing cheek and chin, and a hearty chuckle. When faced with this cheery face every morning, why worry?

Joel's first birthday rolled by, and he still had trouble sitting up without support. Thirteen months, fourteen, fifteen, sixteen, seventeen passed.

The waiting game ended. Our doctor referred us to a pediatric neurologist.

Having no idea what neurologists do, I was surprised when the doctor spent more time interviewing me than examining my son. She spent five minutes maximum with Joel. She peered into his eyes with a flashlight, tested his reflexes with a little hammer, and watched him crawl. Then, while he played at my feet, she sat ramrod straight behind her desk and asked me questions for over an hour.

With an impassive face she informed me that Joel had hypotonia, or low muscle tone. This was probably caused by a lack of oxygen during his birth. Hypotonia, she explained, was a very mild form of cerebral palsy. With time, his muscle tone would improve.

"He may never be an athlete, but he will lead a perfectly

normal life. From what you have told me, I have no reason to suspect any mental impairment. I'd like to continue monitoring him every three months."

"What about physical therapy?" I asked. "Would that speed the healing process?"

"Totally unnecessary," she replied, blinking slowly. "This type of condition takes care of itself with time."

The waiting game. Again.

Even so, my sense of relief filled the room, a palpable presence. Smiling stiffly, the doctor sat half-hidden behind her big desk.

A thought crossed my mind, momentarily marring my exhilaration. This doctor must feel like God. She opened her mouth, pronounced a diagnosis, and with one statement handed me freedom. How often did she hand out life sentences?

I thrust the thought from my mind. After all, this woman was respected in the medical community. Why not trust her?

In celebration, I bought Joel a balloon and an ice cream cone on the way home. I couldn't wait to share the good news with Wally.

Lord, why uncharitable thoughts about this doctor? Do I listen to my instincts, or do I hang onto her gift of freedom with all my strength? I'm tired, Lord. Tired of the nagging worry that forever lurks in the back of my mind. Even though I didn't warm to this woman, I'm giving her my vote of confidence, Lord. Tell me I'm doing the right thing. Amen.

Taking the Plunge

Religion that is
pure and undefiled
before God, the Father,
is this: to care for orphans
and widows in their
distress, and to keep
oneself unstained by
the world.

—James 1:27

The diagnosis of hypotonia calmed my fears considerably. It was tangible, dealing with arms and legs, parts of the body I could see and touch and massage. I kept repeating the neurologist's words to myself, "I have no reason to suspect any mental impairment." Those nine words became my lifeline. I kept my thoughts to myself. Wally, with his perennially optimistic outlook, never seemed to have worried in the first place. During my pregnancy with Joel, Wally and I had thought and prayed about a ministry we could do as a couple. We'd been leaders of our church's junior-senior high youth group for five years, and loved working with teens. One morning when I was three months pregnant, Wally came home with an idea that was to change our lives.

"Kate! What would you think about foster parenting?" His face flushed with excitement, Wally stood in front of the bed, fidgeting. It was a Sunday morning, and I had skipped church to sleep in.

"What? I mean, who? What in the world are you talking about?" Groggy with sleep, I couldn't make sense of his words.

"Us! Foster parents! Wouldn't that be great?"

I groaned. "Whoa! I'm three months pregnant, remember? We have a new baby on the way, not to mention the two wild men wrestling downstairs. What brought this on?"

He explained that board members of a new community venture had presented a program at Adult Education that morning. Plans were underway to open a foster home for troubled teenage girls, and they were looking for houseparents. A husband and wife who had served in a similar capacity in a home for boys shared stories about how the boys had impacted their lives and stretched their faith. While listening, Wally had felt the Holy Spirit's nudging. "It's as if they were talking directly to me," he said.

The conversation ended after I agreed to consider the idea and pray about it. The Holy Spirit hadn't nudged me! My mind was filled with other, more important things. Like what color to paint the nursery, where to buy material for curtains I planned to make, who had the best buy on baby clothes, and how Matt and Justin would react to a new brother or sister.

But the idea never left the back of my mind. It lodged there, nudging me as we established deeper and deeper relationships with the youth at church; nudging me as we took them on a weekend retreat and then on a week-long mission trip; nudging me as I played with Matt and Justin. What happens to those other kids, I wondered. The ones who don't have parents who care enough to play? Or even meet their basic needs? What happens to those kids who've never seen the inside of a church, much less a youth group room? And how about those kids who've been abandoned, given the freedom to roam the streets, and conversely, the life sentence of knowing no one cares? I asked myself if this prodding was from the Holy Spirit or just from my own sense of the world's injustice. The answer to that question remained unclear.

By the time Joel was six months old, the nesting instinct that had so obsessed me during pregnancy began to abate. I began fantasizing about parenting teenage girls. I still had some fears about Joel's development, but the doctor didn't seem unduly worried. Matt and Justin were well-adjusted, and both were in school—Matt in third grade and Justin in first. It wasn't as if I didn't have the time. And there was the commitment Wally and I had made to each other during a Marriage Encounter four years earlier. At that time we had committed our marriage to Jesus Christ, and had pledged to dedicate ourselves as a couple to some type of ministry. Youth group had served that purpose for five years. Was it time to move on to something bigger?

"I feel as if we're getting too comfortable," Wally said one night in bed before we turned off the light. "Look at us. We're living the good life. Money's no problem. We have a wonderful, comfortable home. Sure, the house could be bigger, but hey . . ."

We both laughed. I'd been complaining about lack of closet space for years. I even dreamed about houses that were nothing but closets!

Wally continued. "The boys are growing older, we do the same old stuff at youth group every Sunday night, we meet with our covenant group every other week to study, go to church every Sunday, try and find time for devotions every morning . . ."

"What's wrong with all that?" I protested, perplexed. "Don't you think that's pleasing to the Lord?"

"Sure, but it's too easy! Do you think that's all God wants us to do? Sit at home and be comfortable? What about all the other kids out there? The ones who . . ."

I interrupted. "The ones whose parents don't care? The ones who stay out all night, drinking and doing drugs, with no curfew or parent waiting up for them? The ones who don't know Jesus? I've been thinking about them. More often than I care to!"

"Well, what do you say?" Wally grabbed my hand. "Do you

think we could handle it? Is the Lord calling you to this? I think I'm hearing a real call."

We stared at each other. My stomach fluttered as I reached over, turned out the bedside lamp, and settled myself into the covers. Voice muffled by the pillow, I finally answered.

"I don't know. I'm just not sure."

Shortly after Joel's first birthday, we decided to interview for the position, which was still open. Making the decision was like taking the first swim of the season, when the water's still icy. There's no way to acclimate yourself beforehand—you either jump in and swim or decide the water's too cold.

We took the plunge. The interview went well, and we were offered the job. We signed a one-year contract and began helping the board of directors look for a house. We found a beautiful home with more than enough space for four teenage girls as well as our family. Three months later we found renters for our house and moved into the Parkdale Home for Girls.

Lord, decisions like this never come easy. It's so hard to separate our voice from your voice, our will from your will. You've blessed us so richly, and we can't help but feel this is a great opportunity to return that blessing to the world. I pray the water's not too cold, Lord! Amen.

His Name Is Joel

So out of the ground the Lord God formed every animal of the field and every bird of the air, and brought them to the man to see what he would call them; and whatever the man called every living creature, that was its name.

—Gen. 2:19

While at Parkdale, Joel's second birthday approached, and still he could not walk. Tired of the waiting game, we employed a physical therapist. One Wednesday afternoon I sat on a blue bolster at the edge of the mat and watched the therapist work with Joel. She bounced him on a huge red ball, defining balance reactions. Turning him tummy down on the ball and holding his feet, she rolled him back and forth. Joel's giggle was contagious. Soon Barb and I were laughing too. It was a good session.

Finished, Barb held Joel on her lap and put on his shoes. She looked at me, a frown creasing her forehead.

"Have you thought about enrolling Joel in a preschool?"

"Well, yes." I replied. "With his delays, though, I'm not sure where to take him. He wouldn't be able to keep up with the other kids."

"I'd like to suggest a great preschool for the multihandicapped in your school district. Joel would be with other children with developmental delays. He'd receive physical and occupational therapy, and he'd have a chance to work on socialization. Why don't you think about it?"

Multihandicapped!

The word hit me like a physical blow. I gasped. The curtain I had hung to protect me from my worst fears had been lifted. Silent words formed. Angry words. Fearful words. My child is not handicapped! Don't you dare use those words in the same sentence with my son's name! Developmentally delayed yes, but multihandicapped, never! *No! No! No!*

I tried to remain outwardly calm, not wanting her to witness my terror.

"I'll think about it," I said, noncommittally. Not even pausing to say good-bye, I scooped Joel into my arms and headed toward the door. Once outside, I took a big gulp of fresh air. I would not give power to that label, that name. Using those words might make them come true. That I would not, could not, permit.

Lord, what power a name holds! Far beyond the combination of letters on the page or the sound of the syllables spoken aloud. A name reveals the very essence of our being!

It hurts, Lord, to hear the word handicapped *used in the same breath with my son's name. Oh, how it hurts! I wanted to scream today. I wanted to scream "His name is Joel!" His name is Joel. No matter what else we may discover, help me hold onto that fact, Lord. Amen.*

Difficult Choices

Let my cry come before you, O LORD; give me understanding according to your word!

—Ps. 119:169

Several months into our job as foster parents, I sat down to help Matt with a science project on the solar system. Using construction paper, he had cut out circles of varying size, colored them elaborately to look like the planets, and was ready to paste them onto a large piece of poster board.

I watched him arrange the circles, smallest planet to largest, in a straight line on the white background.

"Don't you think it would be neat to put them around the sun in a circle?" I asked. I moved pieces around for a few minutes, arranging them in the correct configuration.

"I liked it the other way," Matt answered sullenly. He had become moody and uncommunicative over the months since our move.

"But this shows the way the planets are lined up in space," I urged. "See?" I pointed out a page in his science book showing a similar model.

"Oh, all right." He jabbed the bottle of glue onto the back of Mercury, and pounded it into place next to the sun. I gave him a hug.

"That looks great," I said. "You've decorated these planets so realistically. I bet you'll get an 'A'." He squirmed away from my good-night kiss. Too tired to tackle his bad mood, I went up to bed. It was Wally's turn to tuck the boys in.

The next morning on the way down to breakfast, I noticed a pile of crumpled paper in the corner. Investigating, I discovered it was the remains of Matt's poster, torn into several pieces. It was beyond repair.

"Matt!" I bellowed through the doorway. "Get in here right now!"

Matt appeared, a defiant look clouding his face.

"I told you I liked it better the way I did it, and you didn't listen," he said. "You *never* listen anymore. I made a new poster after you went to bed—I made it the way I wanted it. So just leave me alone." Rigid shoulders and flashing eyes spoke of anger and injured pride.

I looked at him in silence. He was right. I didn't listen anymore. Who had time to listen? I had an agenda. I had ideals. I had a plan to change people's lives, make the world a better place to live!

"You're right, Matt," I apologized. "I should have let you do it your own way. It's your project. I should have listened." I gave him a big hug, complimented him on the new poster he'd made, and got everyone off to school without further incident.

I was hovering on the brink of nervous exhaustion. Being a foster mom had proven to be more demanding, both physically and emotionally, than I'd ever imagined. Wally thrived on the challenge, but he was away working most of the time. I longed for the comfortable, old-shoe existence we'd left behind. We both spent endless hours with the girls, listening and counseling, meeting with case workers and school counselors, helping formulate future goals, and doling out discipline when house rules were broken (which happened on a regular basis). The job grew more complicated daily, at a seemingly exponential rate.

What tired me most was the never-ending worry. I worried not only about how the girls were doing presently, but about their futures as well. I worried about their friendships, their grades, the possibility of drugs and sex and pregnancy. I worried about their relationships with their families and the rivalries that were springing up in our family. I worried about Matt's moodiness, Justin's impulsive nature, and Joel's continuing lack of muscle control. There just wasn't enough of me to go around. I seldom spent time with the boys in the evenings, and the weekends were taken up with chores and chauffeuring kids around town. Private time for Wally and me had become conspicuous by its absence.

After weeks of prayer, we made the difficult decision not to sign a contract for another year. Although Wally loved the commotion and chaos that teenagers brought to our lives, he knew we could succeed in the job only as a team. Plagued with sleeplessness, irritability, and a state bordering on panic, I wasn't making a very good teammate.

Although consumed with guilt over my "failure" as a foster mother, I knew my children needed an emotionally healthy mother. And with Joel still crawling at the age of two-and-a-half, we were beginning the round of doctors and therapists again, which was stressful enough.

The timing of our decision, thankfully, couldn't have been better. One of our girls, just eighteen, had moved out on her own. Another had recently been removed by the court. We offered to take the remaining girl with us when we moved back to our own home, but our request was turned down by the Parkdale Board of Directors.

High ideals somewhat tarnished, we packed our belongings and went back to our home on Burnham Street. The experience had taught us much about sacrificial love as well as about our own limitations as human beings. It showed us, in a very real way, that only God is in control, only God can change lives. Although it wasn't made clear to us at the time, that would be the most important lesson of all as we approached the storms that lay just ahead in our lives with Joel.

Dear Lord, your ways are not our ways, that is for certain. We prayed so long and so hard before making the decision to foster parent these girls. It feels like failure to say no to another year. If only we could see what you see. If only we could see the impact we've made in this short time, and the effect that will have on these precious girls' futures. But our vision is so limited. Help us Lord, to have faith without proof. To know that in all things, you, Lord, work for good. Amen.

His Name Is Joel

High-Wire Artist

Have you not known? Have you not heard?
The LORD is the everlasting God,
    the Creator of the
    ends of the earth.
God does not faint or grow weary,
God's understanding is unsearchable.
God gives power to the faint,
    and strengthens the powerless.

—Isa. 40:28–29

I put down the iron and wiped beads of perspiration from my forehead. The church windows, though open wide, offered no relief in the form of a breeze. The air hung motionless, thick with the sticky humidity of mid-July. Yards and yards of royal blue fabric dotted with glow-in-the-dark teddy bears lay unfurled at my feet.

Karianne and Angie, two youth group members, stooped over a nearby table, measuring and cutting material. The iron hissed as I picked it up again, letting it glide back and forth over the fabric. The smell of hot cotton arose with billows of steam. We worked quickly and quietly, anxious to see the end result—new curtains for the church nursery. While we measured, cut, ironed, and sewed, another crew of workers was busy giving the grungy gray walls of the nursery a fresh coat of white paint.

The church corridors overflowed with the noise and vitality of twenty teenagers. Shouts of laughter punctuated the low background noise of young voices, and strains of Christian rock wafted out through open windows. The building reeked of paint.

It was our youth group's annual summer mission trip. The teens had given a week of their summer vacation to work in the name of Christ. Their wages? Simply the satisfaction of a job well done and a week of fellowship and fun. The three previous summers we had helped in neighboring states, but this year we stayed home to give our own church a much needed face-lift. The makeover involved painting the church school wing and making curtains for four classrooms.

A screech from the stairwell caused Karianne, Angie, and me to look up from our work. I ran to the doorway.

"Mrs. Bolduc! come quick!" Tammy, the eighth-grader I had assigned to watch Joel that morning, stood at the top of the stairs, waving her arms and jumping up and down. I ran up the steps two at a time, wondering what catastrophe had struck.

"Is Joel OK?" I asked.

Tammy disappeared around the corner without an answer. I followed at a trot, frantic.

Heart pounding, I ran into the room where I had left the two of them only an hour before, and immediately saw that everything was all right. Joel sat in the middle of the room, toys scattered all about. His face lit up as I entered.

"What's going on, Tammy?" I asked, irritation replacing fear. I struggled to catch my breath.

"Wait til you see this!" she said with a grin. She picked up a foam ball, threw it over her head, and caught it. Joel immediately crawled toward her.

"No crawling, Joel," she admonished. "If you want the ball, you'll have to stand up and walk over here." She dropped to her knees, holding the ball toward him.

"Come on, now. I know you want the ball. Show Mommy what you can do, big guy."

Joel looked at me with a grin on his face. He crawled over to a chair and pulled himself up.

"Ball!" he said, bobbing up and down excitedly.

"Yup! Come on and get it," Tammy encouraged. "Mommy wants to see you walk over here."

I stood in the doorway, arms crossed, holding my breath. Joel was exactly two-and-a-half, and still had not taken his first steps. Six months of physical therapy had succeeded in strengthening his muscles somewhat, but on rough days I still had to fight away visions of wheelchairs.

Joel glanced at me again, the expression on his face serious this time. Tammy kneeled about four feet away from him, the bright yellow ball held out as a bribe. A look of utter concentration wrinkled Joel's brow as he let go of the chair. Both arms windmilled as he fought for balance. Like a high-wire artist he tottered toward her, gaining momentum, until, as a finale, he crashed into her outstretched arms with a squeal of delight.

"Hurrah! Go Joel!" In my concentration I'd failed to notice that several kids had joined me in the doorway, their shouts of encouragements mingling with mine. I laughed and cried at the same time as Joel giggled at all the hullabaloo.

How fitting that this long-awaited milestone should be reached among this group of teens, who had played such an important part in our lives over the preceding five years. Joel had been born into an extended family of young people that accepted and cherished him from the start. In his first month of life he had been passed around, held, hugged, and kissed more than most babies are in their first twelve months. He was a fixture at Sunday night youth group meetings, as well as at weekend retreats. This was his third summer mission trip. The kids had worried almost as much as we did about his developmental delays, so I knew their celebration was as honest and sweet as my own.

Wally slipped into the doorway beside me.

"What's up?" he asked.

I nodded toward the middle of the room where Tammy was picking up the ball again. She lightly bonked Joel's nose.

"Let's play ball, short stop. Show Daddy how to play ball."

Joel's face squished up in concentration as he pulled himself to a standing position. More confident this time, he rapidly stepped forward with one foot, lurching his way across the floor to Tammy. Reaching her, he grabbed the ball and threw it across the room. Giving a loud whoop, Wally whisked Joel off the floor and onto his shoulders. Then, grabbing my hands, he led the three of us in a victory dance down the freshly painted hallway.

Our little boy could walk.

Lord, I praise you for the healing work you are doing within Joel. Help me to remember that you are the everlasting God, the Creator of all, and that you never grow weary. Continue to strengthen me, Lord, with your might and power, even as you continue to strengthen my son. Amen.

When the Righteous Cry for Help

When the
righteous cry for help,
the LORD hears,
    and rescues them
    from all their troubles.
The LORD is near to the
brokenhearted,
    and saves the
    crushed in spirit.
Many are the afflictions
of the righteous,
but the LORD rescues
from them all.
            —Ps. 34:17–19

I watched from behind the curtain as the psychologist parked his car, stepped out, pulled a large black case out of the backseat, and lugged it up our front walk. The man was small, pale, and balding. I disliked him immediately.

I answered the doorbell, however, with a courteous smile and handshake, and led the "inquisitor" to the family room. Joel was nearly three. Baffled by the lack of medical answers for his continuing developmental delays, we had decided to enter the frustrating and frightening world of psychological testing in order to enroll him in the local district's preschool for the multihandicapped.

His tone brisk and businesslike, Dr. Jones suggested we sit at the kitchen table for the testing. He obviously did not feel it important to set Joel or me at ease. Intrigued by the big black bag, Joel sat quietly on my lap.

"Just how long will the testing take?" I asked. "You do take his age into consideration, right? Not many three-year-olds sit still for long."

"Now, don't you worry," Dr. Jones answered. "We've had lots of experience. You just hold him on your lap as best you can, and we'll do the rest."

I wondered who "we" referred to.

I bit my lip and decided not to ask any more questions. Dr. Jones opened the black case, and Joel craned his neck to see what was hiding inside.

The doctor pulled out a doll. It was naked—the plastic kind with moveable arms and legs. The body was smudged with fingerprints.

"Joel, what is this? This is a . . .," the doctor prompted in sugary tones.

Joel ignored the questions and grabbed the doll. He manipulated the arms and legs a few times. Yanking hard, he pulled an arm out of the socket. He laughed and threw it on the floor. Face expressionless, Dr. Jones bent down and retrieved it.

"What is this, Joel? What came off the doll?" He held the arm toward Joel. Joel snatched it and threw it again. Reaching out, Dr. Jones made a neat catch, and put the armless doll and appendage back into the bag.

"OK, Joel. Let's see what else we have here." The doctor plopped down a set of one-inch colored cubes. I winced. Our pediatrician had tested Joel periodically with similar blocks. Joel's fine motor control was so poor that he could rarely stack two blocks successfully.

Confronted with these objects of frustration, Joel stuck out an arm and swiped them off the table in one fluid motion. Unruffled, the doctor got down on his knees and gathered them up. He set them in front of Joel again.

"Let's see if we can make a train with the blocks, Joel," he said sweetly. He made train noises and pushed the line of blocks toward Joel.

"No!" Joel yelled, and once again the blocks went flying helter-skelter. Dr. Jones paused and wrote in a little notebook. He picked up the blocks and put them back into the bag. This time he pulled out a three-piece puzzle. Circle, square, triangle. Knocking the pieces out of the puzzle board, he handed the circle to Joel.

"This is a circle. Can we find the place where the circle goes?"

Frowning over his shoulder at me, Joel took the puzzle piece and chewed on it. *What in the world is going on here?* his expression asked. I reassured him with a hug. The puzzle piece flew over the doctor's head and skidded across the countertop. Again Dr. Jones scribbled in his notebook, and then pulled a book out of the bag.

"I think he might respond better if I ask him the questions," I said hesitantly.

I was rewarded with a patronizing smile. "You can hold the book, but for the test results to be accurate, I must do the questioning."

Joel squirmed out of my lap. I held the book toward him.

"What animal is this, Joel?" the doctor asked, pointing toward a cow.

Joel ran across the room, picked up a stuffed animal, and brought it over to Dr. Jones. He held it out, a peace offering, his most charming smile lighting his face.

"He knows that's a cow," I said, my voice quivering. "And he knows cows say "moo" and ducks say "quack." It's obvious he isn't going to test well. He doesn't *know* you, and he has no reason to *trust* you. Why don't you ask me some questions? I'll tell you what he can and can't do."

Dr. Jones shrugged. "Of course. You can tell me whatever you like, Mrs. Bolduc. But I can't use that information when I score the tests. It is important that I see the behaviors performed. Otherwise, the test results will be skewed." He folded his hands on the table.

You're inhuman, I thought.

I rattled off Joel's accomplishments. The few words he could say, the fact he seemed to understand what we said to him, the toys he played with, toys he avoided, social habits, and so on. The man dutifully penned it all down in his notebook.

The ordeal lasted an hour and a half. By the time I ushered the doctor and his black bag out the door, I felt as though I'd put in a sixteen-hour day.

I turned on Sesame Street, sat in the rocking chair, and patted my lap. Joel ran over and climbed up. We sat and rocked. I held him tight, kissing his soft hair, taking deep breaths, fighting waves of nausea.

"Oh baby," I whispered. "What are we going to do?" Joel giggled with delight at Cookie Monster's antics and snuggled more comfortably against my chest.

I closed my eyes and silently pleaded heavenward. "I will do anything," I implored. "Anything, if you will heal my son. Look at all I've done already, Lord. Eight years of youth work every Sunday night, weekend retreats, week-long mission trips, conferences. Ten years of committee work at church. A year of foster parenting. I'm your servant, Lord. Haven't I made that clear? What else do you want?"

Joel looked up with a giggle. Ernie and Bert were having a pillow fight, and feathers flew everywhere, a snowy cloud.

I turned back to God. "Call me, Lord. Send me. Africa. Asia. The slums of Cincinnati. The slums of Calcutta. I'll work with the terminally ill. AIDS patients. Battered children. Anything. If you will only heal my son."

My pleas were answered only by inner silence and the sound of Sesame Street's closing song.

Two weeks later the doctor's report arrived in the mail. I read it alone, before Wally came home from work.

"Joel Bolduc is a 35-month-old youngster with moderate developmental laps in the general motor area and mild developmental laps in the adaptive behavior area. Joel's ability measures in the moderately retarded range on the Bayley Scale."

Crushed and brokenhearted, I cried out to God. "Deliver us, Lord, from this nightmare!" Wiping away the tears, I told myself the results were incorrect and vowed to do everything in my power to help my child learn, to prove the psychologist wrong.

Lord, your Word tells me that when the righteous cry for help, you deliver them. Have I not proven my faithfulness to you? Have I not said I am willing to do more in your name? I'm holding up my end of the bargain, Lord. Where are you? Amen.

Garments of Praise

The spirit of the
Sovereign LORD is on me,
because the LORD has
anointed me . . .
to proclaim freedom for
the captives . . .
    to bestow on them
    a crown of beauty
    instead of ashes,
the oil of gladness
instead of mourning,
    and a garment of
    praise instead of a
    spirit of despair . . .
    everlasting joy
    shall be theirs.

—Isa. 61:1, 3, 7 (NIV)

It was a muggy May afternoon. I put Joel to bed for his nap and went outside for some blessed rest. It had been a rough day. Five major tantrums in the course of five hours was too much for anyone. Joel's pleasant disposition had undergone a radical transformation. Easily frustrated, he whined and cried often and had begun throwing tantrums regularly. Desperately I tried to pray, but I was too wound up to concentrate. Tears of anger and self-pity wet my face.

As I sat on the back porch, the wind rose. Small branches and bits of leaf and seed hit the porch and the side of the house. A strong gust of wind from the southwest filled the air with white, fluffy dandelion seeds. It was an ethereal sight. Like sticky cotton candy, the seeds covered the ground and clung to my shirt. I sputtered as a piece of fluff found its way into my mouth.

The wind shifted and rose. The stately oak in the side yard, massive of trunk and limb, whipped around like a sapling. Its branches bent almost to the ground. The wind echoed through the woods behind the house with a hoarse roar.

Sheets of mist obscured my view of the woods. A driving deluge of rain from the west chased me into the house to close windows. I ran upstairs to check on my napping son. I could barely open his door. Leaning my shoulder against the wood and pushing hard, I was confronted by a fierce wind.

Joel stood in his crib, head thrown back, blonde hair blowing, facing the westward window. The curtains leapt horizontal into the room, blowing toward him in salute. A tree rapped in staccato on the windowpane. Legs spread wide, hands anchoring him firmly to the side of the bed, Joel faced it like a sailor in a storm.

He stood in total concentration. No trace of fear as his window became a porthole into a mighty ocean of rain. No trace of fear as little balls of ice clinked against the windowpane. No trace of fear as his room filled with a mighty wind that took my breath away. Joy illuminated his face with radiant color, and blue eyes gleamed with excitement.

The force of the wind somehow changed me as well. My heavy and burdened spirit overflowed with praise. The Spirit of the Lord was upon me, anointing me with the oil of joy, clothing me in garlands of beauty.

Lord, I praise you for the gift of your Spirit. That you can replace ashes with beauty, mourning with joy, and a heavily burdened and failing spirit with praise is too wonderful to comprehend. Help me to understand that you are there waiting to transform my spirit, especially in the midst of my despair, my hopelessness, my guilt, and my fear. Amen.

Light Rising in Darkness

If you offer your food
to the hungry
    and satisfy the needs
    of the afflicted,
then your light shall rise
in the darkness
    and your gloom be
    like the noonday.

—Isa. 58:10

Never before had I witnessed such brokenness.

Four-year-old James sat motionless in his wheelchair. He had the face of a cherub in a Renaissance painting. There was one painful difference. This cherub would never fly, or even rise up and walk. Imprisoned by his disabilities, James sat quietly, unable to see, talk, or even move his limbs independently.

Another wheelchair held a child disabled by cerebral palsy. While James sat calmly, Kenny jerked and twitched in an unsyncopated rhythm. Eyes blinking, he struggled to communicate. Loud sighs and groans filled the room. What was going on in his mind? What a nightmare to be trapped by a body unable to communicate. I turned my gaze away.

A third child, Joey, wandered around the room on tiptoe,

randomly picking up toys and setting them down. After several minutes of this, he plopped down in a corner and rocked, staring into space. Tears rolled down his cheeks as he cried without sound.

It was my first visit to our school district's preschool program for multihandicapped children. The psychological testing had taken place in January, and by the following summer it had become apparent that Joel needed professional help that we could not provide for him at home. Temper tantrums were erupting with regularity, he could not concentrate on any task for more than a few moments, and he became frustrated and angry when with his peers. In desperation, we made the difficult decision to enroll him in the preschool program. Although his disability did not appear to be as severe as those of the other children in the class, we had run out of options.

As parents we were expected to visit the classroom for observation once a month. I found returning difficult. With no past exposure to people with profound disabilities, my initial reaction was fear and revulsion. This soon gave way to guilt. How could I feel this way about any of God's children? Pity rose like bile in my throat, leaving me sick with hopelessness.

One morning as I observed through the one-way mirror, the teacher unstrapped and gently lifted James out of his wheelchair. She laid him faceup on an exercise mat, stroked a strand of silky hair back from his forehead, and massaged his temples with her fingertips. A smile danced across James's face, which illuminated his wide green eyes. A beautiful smile. The first I'd seen in three visits.

Pat continued to massage, working her way down his body: shoulders, arms, hands, legs. Taking off his shoes and socks, she rubbed his feet, carefully kneading each toe. This time James smiled with his whole body, wriggling and squirming from head to foot. All the while she spoke to him in low, comforting tones.

I returned home filled with wonder and awe at the joy and love I'd seen reflected in the smile of a severely disabled child. The love and compassion this teacher demonstrated in a simple massage convicted me of my need for a changed attitude. Not only toward the children with severe disabilities in my son's class, but toward my son's disability as well. I was struck with the realization that I was disabled, too. Disabled by fear and ignorance.

No longer a place of fear, the classroom became a place of healing. Light rose up in place of darkness. My vision changing, I saw joy alongside suffering, freedom beneath bondage, and relief beyond pain.

I knew I had many lessons yet to learn as I journeyed toward compassion and acceptance. My child's classroom became my classroom, his teacher my teacher.

Lord, your ways are such a paradox. To be filled, we must first empty ourselves. To experience healing, we must first suffer. To live in the light, we must first know darkness. Thank you for teachers like Pat, who know these truths and pour themselves out for your children. Amen.

Deceived and Abandoned

Why is my
pain unceasing,
my wound incurable,
refusing to be healed?
Truly you are to me like
a deceitful brook,
like waters that fail.

—Jer. 15:18

As the months and seasons passed by in a hazy blur, I found myself struggling daily with a terrible sense of aloneness. A wonderful husband and three sons kept me busy. My mother, brothers, and sister all lived nearby. My husband's parents lived just around the corner. I placed a high priority on my friendships. An active prayer life kept me in touch with God.

Yet, seldom a day passed, even in the midst of my hectic schedule, that I did not feel abandoned and alone. No one, I was sure, not even God, understood the way I felt. No one, not even God, knew how much I hurt.

I talked to my husband, my boys, my friends. I listened. I hugged, admonished and cajoled, kissed hurts away, and tucked my children in at night. But there was no one to kiss this hurt away for me. No one to tuck me in at night and tell me everything would be all right. I found myself asking the same question over and over again. *Are you there, God? Are you listening? How long will I go on hurting? Hurting for my beautiful son?*

Joel's hair-pulling behavior became a major source of discouragement. I could deal with the developmental delays, I thought, but not this. It had begun when he was three. Now four, his behavior had taken a turn for the worse.

His physical therapist wore a bathing cap during therapy sessions. She was afraid of his hands. I no longer invited friends with children into our home. Joel could not keep his hands to himself. We avoided playgrounds. Church was a nightmare. The children expected Joel to pull hair, and he obliged. They ran the other way when they saw him approaching. Church school teachers did not know how to handle the situation. No one invited us to visit.

I prayed, pleaded, begged. Please Lord . . . please . . . please . . . please. I was ashamed of the whining quality of my prayers, but could not help myself. *Are you there, God? Are you listening? How long will I go on hurting? Hurting for my beautiful son?*

I resented being a prisoner in my own home. One rainy day, I zipped Joel into his raincoat for a drive to my friend Patty's house. The visit started off well. Megan, age two, and Wesley, age four, sat on the floor, playing with Legos. Joel joined them, and Patty and I sat on the couch and sipped tea, talking as the kids played. My heart began to lift. Maybe things would go okay today.

A loud scream ripped through the air. I looked up to see Joel pulling Megan by the hair, caveman style, across the floor. He laughed as he pulled. Rushing over, I crouched down and began disentangling Joel's fingers from Megan's hair with difficulty. My heart pounded in my ears, competing with Megan's screams. Every time I pried one finger loose another grabbed on more tightly.

"Let go!" I screamed. "Let go of her hair! You're hurting her!"

Finally, prying his fingers loose, I dragged him over to the corner. By this time I was panting with the exertion as well as with anger.

"Sit there until I tell you to get up," I ordered and sat down on the couch where Patty was comforting Megan on her lap. I reached out and patted her shoulder.

"I'm sorry, Meggie. Joel didn't mean to hurt you. He doesn't know how much that hurts."

Suddenly something snapped inside my soul. An inner voice screamed: *This is too much, God. Why is my son hurting other people? What makes him do this?*

Megan stopped crying and watched with interest as ragged sobs erupted from deep within me. Joel stared wide-eyed from the corner. Patty put her free arm around my shoulder and began praying. Even in the midst of all this attention, I felt terribly alone.

Are you there, God? Are you listening? How long will I go on hurting? Hurting for my beautiful son?

Dear Lord, help me find comfort in your Word. As I read, I see that I am not alone; that even your prophets and psalmists felt deceived and abandoned. On days such as this, I know I could not take one step further without your assistance. Dear Jesus, I fall at your feet in supplication. Forgive my doubts, my whining, and crying. Forgive my pitiful, pleading prayers and fill me with prayers of faith. I read further into your Word and find this passage in Jer. 31:13: "I will turn their mourning into joy, I will comfort them, and give them gladness for sorrow." Open me to your comforting presence, Lord. Knock down the walls of doubt so that I might truly believe. Amen.

I Lie Awake

I lie awake. Even though Wally lay next to me, gently snoring, I felt completely, utterly alone. No one intercepted the scavenger thoughts that lived off my pain. Even God had gone, his face hidden from me.

I felt the heat of Wally's body, warm as toast on a winter night. Once upon a time we had snuggled in the cold of winter. Now I clung to the edge of the bed, a high four-poster. I could have easily fallen to the floor, but that would have been preferable to any person, including my husband, penetrating my pain. Who knew what this flood wall, if torn down, would allow to escape? And so scavenger thoughts roamed at will, feeding off my misery, freely tearing down self-esteem, hope, and joy. I was left only with emptiness and a nagging, undefined fear.

I tossed and turned through the night. Wally reached out for me and I stiffened, fending off his embrace with a sharp elbow. Scooting further toward the edge of the bed, I looked down at the floor. A full moon shone through the window, illuminating clothes piled in the corner, a box of unmatched socks sticking out from under the dresser, and towels from that morning's shower heaped next to the door.

The mess was a potent symbol of my life. In my depression, I couldn't accomplish anything. Dirty laundry piled up; dirty dishes littered countertops; stacks of unopened mail cluttered the kitchen. The boys came home from school to find a mother dull with depression. I was on a downward spiral. The knowledge that Joel's "delays" were much more than delays was knowledge I was not ready to accept. His behavior problems worsened by the day, and my gloom deepened.

Wally mumbled something unintelligible, and I fumed at his ability to sleep. Who was this stranger sharing my bed? We had been married for sixteen years, and yet somehow were further apart than the night we met. At least then there had been smiles and laughter, a gentle hug and good-night kiss. Where had the affection gone, the desire to share our hopes and dreams and fears? Where was the Christ we had put at the center of our marriage just five short years before?

I lie awake. Like the psalmist's image of a lonely bird on a housetop, I was alone. My inner life looked like the moon shining through the window—barren, cold, and lifeless. Unable to give off warmth or light of its own volition.

I lie awake.

Where are you, Lord? Why do you hide your face from me in the day of my distress? My children need me, my husband needs me, yet I have nothing to give. I am near despair as I fight these fears about Joel. Walled inside myself, I cry out to you in anguish, but you do not answer. Why?

Deceived by Pride

Your proud heart
has deceived you . . .

—Obad. 3:1

Leaving Joel in front of the television watching Sesame Street, I carried a load of laundry down the basement steps. Quickly sorting through darks and lights, I heard the thump of Joel's footsteps overhead, and then a crashing chord from the piano. I breathed a sigh of relief as I threw towels into the washing machine. If he was playing the piano, I reasoned, the rest of the house was safe from his restless hands.

Our days were strewn with mishaps.

I left the room for a minute to go to the bathroom, and Joel coated the carpet next to his bed with Vaseline.

I ran outside with a bag of trash, and he ripped up two library books.

The phone rang. I answered it, leaving him alone in the family room for a minute or two. He trashed the entire room.

I started dinner. Joel played quietly. Engrossed in the recipe, I failed to see that he'd opened the refrigerator door. I looked up to watch him dump an entire gallon of milk over the shelves below.

Dinner burned on the stove as I wiped up the mess.

At the grocery store, Joel leaned out of the cart, swiping cans off the shelves. I spent half my shopping time retrieving merchandise from the floor. Unable to concentrate, I returned home with two bags of groceries rather than four.

It was nearly impossible to keep up with the laundry. I dared not leave Joel alone, even at the age of four, for more than a minute. The five minutes needed to change a load often proved disastrous.

As my foot hit the top step, the thick, powerful smell of excrement assaulted my nostrils. All was quiet. I cringed.

"Joel? Where are you? Joel!"

He was in the living room, diaper off, decorating the piano with a bowel movement. My grand piano. My if-you-could-save-just-one-thing-if-your-house-caught-on-fire piano. He stood naked on the piano bench, reaching in over the top with dirty hands. The keys were painted with streaks of brown, and the piano's shiny black sides resembled a kindergarten finger painting. I caught him in the act of smearing the inner strings.

The stench was overwhelming. I retched. Hearing me, Joel turned around, a gleeful smile greeting the mask of shock that must have transformed my face.

Shock kindled into rage. My stiff mask gave way to fury. Grabbing Joel's arm, I whisked him onto the floor and planted a spank on his bare leg. I pulled him up the steps, wiped him down with a damp washcloth, and threw him into the tub. My stony silence gave way to screams of anger. Joel looked up at me uncomprehendingly.

I knew, deep in my heart, that he absolutely did not know why I was screaming. Still, I could not help myself.

After drying and redressing him, I gathered together a pail of water, Murphy's Soap, and a rag. Gagging, I attacked the mess. It took a full hour. Joel watched from the couch. I dared not look at him. Just the sight of him made my blood boil.

I opened windows to rid the house of the awful smell and stood looking out, trying to collect myself. The voice of reason murmured in my ear.

Call Wally.

Call your mother.

Call a friend.

You need help.

Pride whispered burning words in my other ear. Sibilant words. Hissing words.

You're so stressed out you must ask for help?

You admit you're unable to handle this situation yourself?

Someone else must come in and see the mess you've created?

You're not strong enough, self-sufficient enough to take care of your own problems?

I succumbed to the message. Day by day, pride grew stronger within me. Reason battled weakly, its voice overcome by one more powerful.

I spent hours arguing with myself over whom to ask for help. Hours lifting the phone and setting it down again. Hours in internal dialogue, just trying to make it through endless days.

Wally doesn't understand. He can't help.

No one else will know how to handle him.

Let someone see this messy house? No!

Admit defeat? Never!

Meanwhile, I grew smaller and smaller within my own eyes.

Too weak to handle the situation, yet too weak to ask for help.

Too proud to admit defeat, yet living a defeated life.

Too proud even to pray.

The battle waged on, my mind the battleground, my sanity the loser. On the outskirts of the skirmish stood my child, my husband, my family, my God.

Listening to the sibilant voice of pride, I ignored them all.

I would handle this situation myself, if it killed me in the doing.

Lord, Lord, Lord, I cannot pray. The words will not come. All I can do is call your name. Hear my cry, Lord. Hear my cry.

From the Precipice

At an acceptable time,
O God,
   in the abundance of
   your steadfast love,
   answer me.
With your faithful help
rescue me from sinking
in the mire . . .
Do not let not the flood
sweep over me,
   or the deep swallow me up,
   or the Pit close its
   mouth over me.
                  —Ps. 69:13–15

The phone rang. I answered it. It was a phone call I'll never forget.

Pat, a friend from church, called to ask about our next Bible study meeting. We talked a moment, and then the conversation turned to Joel. She knew the struggles involved in raising a child with disabilities; her oldest son, now grown, had a learning disability.

"Things aren't going so great," I told her. I launched into a long list of our latest challenges. Hairpulling, tantrums, short attention span, the constant watchfulness Joel required, Matt and Justin vying for my attention, the growing distance between me and Wally.

I absentmindedly cleaned the kitchen countertop as we talked. Pat sympathized, and then veered off in a new direction.

"My boss's son is mentally retarded, and he is the nicest young man. We had them over for dinner last week, and we were so impressed with him! His family loves him to death. He's made such a difference in their lives."

I yawned. It was 10 p.m., and it had been a long day.

"I guess the mental retardation was caused by jaundice. High bilirubin count, or something."

The sponge dripped greasy water onto the floor as my hand stopped in midair.

"I just wanted you to know that there are some success stories out there. I'd love to introduce you to Jimmy sometime. Kathy, are you still there?"

I pulled myself back to reality, wrung out the sponge, and ended the conversation clumsily. I hung up the phone and stood looking into the darkness outside the kitchen window. My reflection peered back, blank-faced. Numbness crept through my skull and down the back of my neck. I shivered. It felt as though someone had injected my brain with Novocaine.

Jaundice. Brain damage. I'd never heard the words used together. Mental retardation. My worst fear. So far I'd successfully blocked out the school's psychological report. Our pediatrician, neurologist, and physical therapist all used the term *developmentally delayed*. We'd been told the problems were most probably caused by a lack of oxygen during birth.

This conversation was the bomb that blew a hole in the carefully constructed walls separating Wally and me. Up until this point, we had battled our separate ways through grief over Joel's failure to develop normally.

Our relationship and marriage is built on the old adage "opposites attract." Wally sees life as an adventure. Each new day holds out limitless possibilities. He's worked hard to make positive thinking a way of life. Negative thoughts are banished before they establish a foothold. A risk taker, Wally takes on new challenges with gusto. Energetic and fun-loving, he's a party waiting to happen.

On the other hand, I sit and think about the day before going out to meet it. Even then, I meet it halfway, with reservations. My view of the world isn't as friendly as Wally's. I treasure quiet moments alone and think things through before making decisions. While Wally is logical and goal oriented, I am intuitive and creative.

Imagination is my greatest strength, but also my greatest weakness. My mind delights in thinking up worst-case scenarios. Scary visions of the future littered my brain. What if we had to institutionalize him? I might have a nervous breakdown. What about Matt and Justin? How would they survive without me? I kept all these thoughts inside until I worked myself up to panic level. Only then did I want to talk. To my husband.

Wally, who didn't allow himself to think too deeply about Joel's problems, had no such desire. Putting all his energy into warding off fearful thoughts, he reacted to my tortured imaginings with disgust. He refused to say anything negative about Joel at all, perhaps afraid that talking about the fears would make them real.

Seeking solace and shelter from my now out-of-control thought life, I found none. A deep canyon ran smack down the middle of our marriage.

Because of his nature, Wally responded to the stress with activity. Not even taking time for lunch, he threw himself into his work. He never sat still. Weekends were jam-packed with activities. Youth group. Hikes in the country with Matt and Justin. Family camping trips. Nights out with the guys. The only time he sat still was late at night when he relaxed in front of the TV, smoking cigarette after cigarette.

On the other hand, the stress left me limp and lifeless with depression, unable to make simple decisions. I awoke in the morning feeling no more rested than when I'd gone to bed. Naps became my lifeline to sanity. Sleep was the only escape from fears that held me captive.

Joel's developmental problems acted like a fun-house mirror, reflecting our personality differences in wildly distorted ways. Day by day, we looked across the table at a mate we no longer recognized. All we had learned from each other, all we had valued in each other, all we'd been attracted to in each other, fell victim to the chasm dividing us. We viewed each other warily from opposite sides of a deep gash running through the fabric of our relationship. The canyon walls were built of denial, deception, selfishness, pride, distrust, and anger.

Neither of us knew how to climb the steep and slippery cliffs. We lived in separate worlds, both of us hurting, both of us dying inside, both of us wanting so badly for the other to reach out with love.

A simple phone call changed everything. Dropping the bomb of new information, it made denial a luxury we could no longer afford. However painful, we had to bridge the gap between us if our relationship was to survive. The healing to come hovered a long way in the distance, invisible beyond thick walls of smoke and flame and ashes.

Lord, rescue us from this pit of denial and despair. We both call out to you privately, in our own ways. Yet we need each other desperately. Help us knock down these walls that divide us. Amen.

Be Angry, but Do Not Sin

Be angry but do not sin; do not let the sun go down on your anger, and do not make room for the devil.

—Eph. 4:26–27

Anger. Slow burning, smoldering, hidden anger. Anger nursed and tended in secret, waiting to explode.

Looking back to the years before Joel's diagnosis, I wonder that our marriage survived. The sun had set on my anger not once, but daily. Going to bed angry had become a way of life.

Angry with everybody and everything, I gave Satan plenty of opportunity to wreak havoc in my home.

I was angry with God, first of all, for allowing my son's disability. I loved my son with my life. I had held him for countless hours, nursed him, rocked him, prayed over him. How could a loving God allow such a travesty—a beautiful boy with a damaged brain?

I was angry with myself, and constantly chastised myself for not coping. Where was my creativity, my stamina, my ability to handle any situation? Fatigue, grouchiness, and lack of patience became constant, unwelcome companions.

Even Joel bore the brunt of my anger. I hated his tantrums, his short attention span, his constant neediness. One day I calculated that his five-minute attention span required ninety-six activities in an eight-hour day. Activities I had to come up with. It was impossible. I raged at the unfairness.

There were times I despised my husband. His platitudes about keeping a positive attitude, his denial of Joel's delays, and his evening pep talks, intended encouragement. I resented it all.

"You go to work every morning," I raged. "You've never even met the physical therapist or the neurologist. When was the last time you were in Joel's classroom? You don't know the strain I'm under. I feel like I'm handling this whole thing by myself. Save the positive thinking stuff for somebody else. I've heard enough."

My words were met with an icy stare and silence.

The anger spilled over into my relationships with Matt and Justin, now ages eight and ten. Why were they acting like kids, for goodness sake? Couldn't they see me struggling? Why didn't they grow up and help out?

My anger spread like a cancer, threatening to consume not only me but the entire family. Everyone grew short-tempered and inconsiderate.

My anger betrayed itself through body language—clenched jaw, folded arms, scowling demeanor. Consumed with dark, ugly thoughts, I found it hard to talk about anything pleasant. When Wally walked in the door after work each night, I shoved Joel toward him. In detail, I recounted all the tantrums he had thrown, all the messes he had made. I said nothing of the cuddling, the loving, the giggles and fun we'd had early in the day. Fatigue and bitterness erased my memory of the good moments.

The tension reached unbearable proportions. One night after dinner, Wally and I sat alone at the kitchen table.

Wally's voice interrupted my thoughts.

"It's obvious you don't love Joel. Why don't you find a babysitter and go to work? He'd be better off with someone else."

Oh, the anger! Red, hot, lava-like anger! Angry words, bitter words welled up within me and spewed across the table.

"What do you know of love? You're gone all day. You have no idea how much love I give this child. I give everything to him! There's nothing left by the end of the day. There's certainly no more left for you. I'm leaving."

We both stood at the same moment. Wally held a half finished glass of milk. Suddenly his hand jerked toward me. I gasped at the cold, wet impact. Milk dripped down my face onto my sweater.

"You deserved it" he pronounced.

Without thinking, I threw my wine glass across the room. It shattered on the far wall, shards of glass scattering everywhere, wine running in rivulets down the wall.

Shaking, I gathered my purse and keys, slamming the front door as I left.

It was two weeks before Joel's fourth birthday. The birthday Wally and I had set as the time for Joel to "catch-up" with his peers.

The dream lay in shattered fragments of glass and the sour remains of spilled milk. The sin of anger burbled within both of us, threatening to destroy everything it touched.

What an ugly memory, Lord. When it resurfaces in my mind, it's like opening an old wound. How did our marriage survive?

It took counseling. It took forgiveness. It took learning to express our repressed anger in appropriate ways. Most of all, it took love to bring us through that terrible time, marriage intact. I thank you, Lord, for the power of love. Agape love. Love that bears all things.

So often I need to learn lessons not once, but a thousand times. This is one of them. Teach me what it means to be angry without sinning, Lord. Teach me again that our anger is normal when we face the dilemma of disability. But, Lord, help me release frustration and rage before the sun goes down. Amen.

Forgiveness

Be on your guard!
If another disciple sins,
you must rebuke the
offender, and if there is
repentance, you must
forgive. And if the same
person sins against you
seven times a day, and
turns back to you seven
times, and says, "I repent,"
you must forgive.

—Luke 17:3–4

Rocked out of denial by our dinner table explosion, Wally and I watched as the walls we had erected tumbled down in great heaps around us. The reconstruction job proved too vast and complicated to undergo alone. We sought out a Christian counselor.

Sitting in the counselor's office with an objective listener freed us to begin a dialogue. Lines of communication, long down, began carrying messages back and forth. It was painful, listening to each other. Difficult and distressing. Sometimes excruciating.

I listened as Wally named my shortcomings as Joel's mother. I did not love him enough, praise him enough, work with him enough, get involved at school enough. I did not spend enough time looking for specialists and consulting with doctors.

He listened as I vented my rage over the fact that his denial kept him from giving me the support I needed, kept him from accompanying me to all the doctors and therapists, kept him from conferences and observation times at Joel's school.

We listened to each other's pain as we talked of guilt and despair and hopelessness. We talked of fatigue and anger and blame. We talked of God, our struggle in prayer, and our fear of losing faith.

It took several weekly sessions before we found a pattern of meaning in the rubble of emotion and cruel words. Accusations and recriminations, angry words, and hurtful memories made returning each week difficult.

As Wally poured out his heart in that sunlit office, I understood for the first time that his anger toward me was displaced anger. His true anger was with himself. Anger that as a man, as a father, he could not fix one of the most important things in his life that needed fixing—his son.

"It's unbearable," he said one day. "Nothing works—none of my old standbys in times of trouble: positive thinking . . . prayer . . . faith . . . inner strength. None of it helps Joel, and none of it helps me. It makes me so angry. I can't tell you how angry it makes me."

For the first time in his life, Wally had experienced total helplessness. Rather than admit this, he shoved the pain and hurt deep inside. Needing an outlet, it eventually boiled over in anger against the safest target—me.

For the first time, I admitted that I'd been nursing a grudge against Wally ever since the jaundice scare of Joel's infancy. I so resented what I saw as his indifference to my pain and fear that I could no longer distinguish those times when he reached out with love. I ignored his good advice, encouragement, and offers of help. I had convinced myself that he had no desire to help; that his insensitivity to the problem was insurmountable. That he didn't care.

Finally the blaming stopped. Freed at last from denial, Wally allowed himself to feel his pain, which made him more sensitive to mine. Unburdened of my resentment, my vision of Wally shifted. As if viewing him through a kaleidoscope, I saw a new pattern emerge. The husband I had viewed as insensitive and uncaring was really a man struggling with intense inner turmoil.

The healing process began as we left the counselor's office one Friday afternoon and, sitting in the car, cried in each other's arms.

"I'm so sorry," I sobbed. "I never realized how you were feeling. You did such a good job of hiding it . . ."

Wally reached over and wiped my cheek with his thumb. "I did a good job of hiding it from myself. Can you ever forgive me for being so insensitive?"

We listened to each other with new ears and heightened sensitivity. Most important, we forgave each other. We admitted our sins, our lack of agape love, our building of walls. We asked each other for forgiveness.

Only through repentance and forgiveness could the healing begin in earnest. Bridge building is hard work. It takes perseverance, patience, and an ability to forgive over and over again. We vowed to quit stuffing feelings, to dialogue daily, and to recommit our love for each other.

Replacing our marriage at the center of our family and Christ at the center of our marriage were two of the most important actions we took. We made a decision to view Joel's disability realistically and to work toward healing and wholeness within ourselves and within our family.

The reconstruction of our marriage had begun.

Lord, your grace is amazing. I thank you for your perfect plan of marriage and family, and I especially thank you for our marriage. Guide us as we struggle to keep talking, as we learn to express our anger appropriately, as we parent this child who is such a challenge. Free us to ask for help when we need it, Lord. And that may be often. Amen.

Your Child Is Not Welcome Here

People were bringing little children to him in order that he might touch them; and the disciples spoke sternly to them. But when Jesus saw this, he was indignant and said to them, "Let the little children come to me; do not stop them; for it is to such as these that the kingdom of God belongs."

—Mark 10:13–14

I balanced a cup of coffee in one hand, and a stack of youth books in the other. My friend Amy, home from the Peace Corps, stood with me outside Fellowship Hall. People, jostling us on their way to the coffee table, interrupted our conversation with hugs, handshakes, and loud greetings. This church took fellowship seriously, and the best part of Sunday morning was the half hour between worship and Sunday school.

"Kathy!"

Hearing my name, I looked around to see the Sunday school administrator, face flushed and chest heaving, charging down the hallway toward us.

Amy laughed. "Uh oh. Looks serious!"

The woman shouldered her way through the crowd, stopping in front of us. Breathing hard, she attempted to regain her composure. The attempt failed.

"Joel is not welcome in the nursery in the future," she barked. "You'll have to make other arrangements for the worship hour. I'm sorry, but he's hurting the other children, and he's impossible to deal with. If you need help setting something up, call me. I'll be in my office Monday and Tuesday." She heaved a big sigh and retreated toward the Sunday school wing.

"Oh my God," Amy whispered. "I don't believe I just heard that."

Clinking coffee cups and hushed voices gradually filled the silence. Someone laughed uneasily, and the noise level returned to normal. I stared at the woman's retreating back.

Not welcome? Not welcome?

Other arrangements during worship? Like what?

Why hadn't the babysitter in the nursery told me the problem was getting worse? I asked her every week. Had she been lying?

Why couldn't she control him? He was only five and she was an adult, for goodness sake!

I talked to the babysitter. Yes, she said, he'd been pulling hair. She hadn't thought the situation serious, but some parents were complaining and wouldn't leave their children if Joel was there.

After that, our older boys took turns staying with Joel in the nursery. I noticed children talking behind their hands when Joel arrived on Sunday mornings. "Oh no! Here comes Joel! Hide!" "Don't let him pull my hair!"

I talked to his Sunday school teacher.

"He won't behave," she said, "so I hold him on my lap the entire hour. It seems to help, but of course it means he doesn't participate."

When asked to volunteer once a month as special helpers with Joel during worship hour, people said no. "I don't have time." "I have too many other responsibilities in the church right now." "I can't miss my worship time."

Looking for volunteers, I called members of the youth group. Joel's behavior had become so unpredictable that none of them felt comfortable watching him anymore. I talked to the babysitter, the Sunday school teacher, and potential volunteers about Joel's behavioral problems and how to handle them. All the same overwhelming responsibilities I dealt with twenty-four hours a day, seven days a week. Was it too much to ask my church for one hour of peace a week?

Anger fermented within me. My thoughts about the church grew horns. When I discussed the problem with Amy or my husband Wally, mean-spirited and ugly words spouted from my mouth.

The church. Meant to be an agent of transformation in a broken world. Where were the love, the compassion, the hope Jesus Christ holds out to us through one another?

To its credit, the church responded in a pragmatic manner.

"We'll form a committee," the Christian education director said.

"We'll have a meeting with interested parties," the education committee promised.

"We'll consider hiring a professional to work with Joel," a well-wisher suggested.

I don't want to form a committee, I screamed inside.

I don't want to hire a professional!

Reach out and hold me!

Pray with me!

Pray for Joel!

Show my son love and compassion, and accept him for who he is.

I'm scared, people!

I don't know what's happening here. I don't understand Joel's developmental delays, his behavior problems.

I'm exhausted. I'm losing my faith. I'm afraid of losing my mind.

I need the family of God to reach out and hold me!

Instead, the church formed a committee. I was put in charge of finding volunteers, providing training, setting up schedules. A tide of ill feeling washed over me. My screams were silent screams. I lost the ability to forgive and forget.

After eight years of membership, we left a church that had played a large part in our journey toward faith.

Only God knows how much that hurt.

Lord, take away the anger and bitterness that are locked in my heart's memory. And help the church be the church. Amen.

Abundant Comfort

Blessed be the God and Father of our Lord Jesus Christ, the Father of the mercies and the God of all comfort, who comforts us in all our affliction, so that we may be able to comfort those who are in any affliction, with the comfort with which we ourselves are comforted by God. For as we share abundantly in Christ's sufferings, so through Christ we share abundantly in comfort too.

—2 Cor. 1:3–5 (RSV)

A great weight lifted from my shoulders the day I told our pastor we were leaving. At the same time, telling him was one of the hardest things I've ever done. Stammering my way through a list of reasons, I ended with a lame cliché.

"Too many bridges have been burned behind us, Thom. We just can't go back to the way it used to be—to the time before Joel. There's too much hurt."

Thom understood better than most. His son, who is Joel's friend, also has multiple disabilities. Thom's wife, Bonnie, is a close friend of mine. We offer each other support very few know how to give. They were new to the church, and leaving them felt like a betrayal.

We spent several Sundays visiting area churches. One Wednesday morning I received a phone call from a woman at the church we'd been to the previous week.

"Hi! My name is Mary Grant, and I'm calling to say how happy we were to have you worship with us last Sunday. I wondered if I could answer any questions for you." Her voice was bright and chirpy, perfect for phone evangelism, I thought wryly.

With several errands and a grocery trip planned, I didn't have time to talk. Besides, I hadn't cared for the freewheeling, informal worship style at this particular church. Meaning to answer "no," I surprised myself by asking a question.

"We have a five-year-old son with mental retardation. Because of behavior problems, he's had a hard time fitting into Sunday school programs. How would your church handle this?"

"There are several children here with disabilities," she said. "Somehow we always find the volunteers we need. The children attend Sunday school with their peers and a special helper." She paused. "What's your son's name?"

"Joel."

"I'd like to pray for Joel. Do you mind if we do that right now, over the phone?"

The offer stunned me. Never had anyone offered to pray with me on the phone.

"Sure," I answered hesitantly.

"Lord, I pray that you would anoint Joel, covering him with the power of your Holy Spirit. I pray that you would lay a healing hand on him, and on his family. Give his parents patience, Lord, and courage to deal with problems as they arise. And Lord, I would ask that you lead them to the right church, a church that can minister to their individual needs. Amen."

Moved by this stranger's concern, I found it hard to speak. I echoed her amen, thanked her for calling, and said good-bye. Sipping my coffee, I stared out the French doors and reflected on the times people had offered to pray with me about Joel.

Very few memories surfaced.

Although I had not liked this church's style, the phone call crystallized in my mind what I did want in a church. I wanted to be part of a community of faith where people were not afraid to pray out loud for one another. A place where a spirit of boldness for the Lord empowered people, snuffing out timidity, forcing growth. A place to receive comfort as well as to give comfort.

The next week a gentle nudging led us across town to yet another church. The Holy Spirit's presence pervaded the entire service. Hymns of praise lifted joyously, prayers of confession rang true, and the teaching was sound biblical truth.

The service ended with a time of healing. Vials of oil in hand, elders stood positioned around the sanctuary. As the congregation stood singing praise songs, a few people went forward for anointing, a laying on of hands, and prayers for healing. By the end of the fourth song, at least one hundred people had gone forward for prayer.

The Spirit of the Lord welled up within me. Cleansed by its healing power, tears fell, washing away anger, hurt, and self-pity. The arm of God encircled my shoulders like a shawl, bringing comfort and a deep feeling of peace. I looked over at Wally. His face, too, was wet with tears. Our hands reached out simultaneously, our fingers intertwining.

I firmly believe God leads us to certain people and places. Neither the stranger's phone call and prayer earlier that week, nor the nudging to attend this church on this particular Sunday, had been an accident. Of that I was certain.

"Yes, Lord," I whispered. "This is where you want us to be."

Anticipation bubbled up within me. Great things would happen here.

Lord, a glimmer of understanding shines within my heart. If I but open myself to you, make myself wholly available to you, listen for your voice and act on it, you will lead me in the way I should go. I have cried out

to you for so long, Lord. I know you have heard my voice. Thank you for your gentle, insistent nudgings. Thank you for leading us to this place of abundant comfort. And help us be comforters, as well as the comforted. Amen.

The Refiner's Fire

And I will . . .
refine them as one
refines silver,
and test them as gold
is tested.
They will call on
my name,
and I will answer
them. I will say,
"They are my
people";
and they will say,
"The LORD is our God."
—Zech. 13:9

On a cold January day, God thrust us headfirst into the fire.

Wally and I sat in the psychologist's office in silence. The doctor's words still rang in the air. "Moderate mental retardation." Nothing prepares a parent for words of this nature. We had seen, yet had not seen; had heard, yet had not heard; had known, yet had not known. Joel's bright-eyed beauty, impish grin, and insatiable curiosity had blinded us to the reality of the situation.

In an instant, a doctor's words had changed our lives. Oh, Joel was the same. The words did nothing to alter his intellectual level or hard-to-manage behavior. The mundane details of day-to-day living changed very little with the diagnosis.

But my husband and I began an invisible, inward transformation in that drab, yellow-walled hospital room. The words of a professional allowed God to begin His refining work in earnest that day.

It was the testing psychologist who mentioned God's refining fire. In his quiet voice, Dr. Dave made a statement I resented at the time, but clung to later.

"The Lord is refining you like silver or gold. I know you can't see past your anguish right now, but he is using this pain to mold you into stronger people, better parents."

Wally did not appear to hear Dr. Dave's words. He sat hunched forward, hands covering his face. Devastated. I sat stoic and strong, arms folded, legs crossed. No more tears remained. In the months and years preceding the testing, I'd cried myself dry. I knew more fully than Wally knew. I felt only a chilly numbness spreading through my body.

I observed my thoughts dispassionately, as if they were someone else's. My face felt wooden. Thoughts floated through the room. I didn't know whose thoughts they were. They whispered, *This must be what hell is like. Or death. A terrible, numbing, nothingness.*

Oh God, please help us! My scream, sent across leaden January skies to an invisible God, was silent. The thoughts kept up their insistent whispering. *Who is this God who uses fire and pain to mold His people? How dare He use a beautiful boy as an object lesson in patience and forbearance?*

In the silence of shock, I watched my husband crumble and break in that room. I held him in the car as he sobbed out his pain before we drove home.

"What are we going to do? What are we going to do?" he repeated over and over until my head throbbed with the rhythm of his words.

I stroked his hair and answered the only way I could.

"I don't know, honey. But it will be all right. We'll make it all right."

I will never forget the depth of that pain. It cut my heart in shreds. I sat alone in the kitchen later that afternoon, waiting for Wally to return from the long walk he had taken through the woods behind the house. I, too, wondered what we were going to do. Would everything really and truly be all right?

It is impossible, while burning, to envision the creature that will emerge from the other side after the fire burns itself out.

Only now can I look back to that day and know with certainty that God heard me call His name in anguish from that dingy hospital room. He molds me still, as He molds my husband, ever closer to the perfect image He has in mind for us.

God has graced me with the vision of how far I have come in this molding process.

But with that vision comes the realization of how far I have yet to go.

Dear Lord, I thank you for your servant, Dr. Dave, who with a few words planted a seed within a grieving mother. How often his words about your refining fire have given me strength. I praise you for the wisdom of your ways, even though they are far beyond my under-standing. Thank you for healing my anger and for opening my eyes to the wholeness that exists within my son despite his disability. Thank you for continually remolding me into the person you would have me become. Amen.

Victory in Tribulation

Rejoice in your hope, be patient in tribulation, be constant in prayer.

—Rom. 12:12 (RSV)

We prayed in the car before entering the special education supervisor's office. My stomach churned, giving me heartburn. I hated confrontation.

We'd come to talk about Joel's transition from preschool to elementary school. The year was off to a disastrous start, Joel's behavior out of control. Almost all gains made through two years of preschool had been lost, and it was already November. I'd talked for hours on the phone with his teacher, with our behavioral psychologist, and with the special education supervisor. Nothing had helped. Joel's behavior worsened daily.

Communication sheets from the teacher had reported excellent behavior the first two weeks of September. The third week had brought a few reports of hair pulling. The fourth week's notes overflowed with reports of tantrums, hair pulling, and grabby hands.

At the teacher's request, I had not visited the classroom until the first week of October. She had said she wanted a chance to develop a routine and let everyone settle in before encouraging visitors. Since Joel usually misbehaved when I visited his classroom anyway, I agreed.

By the first of October something was terribly wrong. Joel had loved preschool, and although his behavior was far from perfect, his teachers expected him to do his best, and he worked hard to please them. He had arrived home from school full of smiles and hugs. Now he stumbled off the bus tired and cranky, whining and misbehaving until bedtime.

It was time for a visit to the classroom

I had been so full of hope for this year. I had envisioned Joel learning his colors and the letters in his name, perhaps part of the alphabet. I was shattered when I discovered Joel had little chance of learning anything in his new school environment.

Three pages of notes documented all I observed that day. Inconsistent response to inappropriate behavior, little or no praise for good behavior, and lack of communication between teacher and aide, resulting in mixed messages to the children. A messy, noisy, and chaotic atmosphere contributed to the confusion.

Joel, like most children with disabilities, thrives on praise and needs consistent discipline. Receiving neither, he lost his ability to function. His brain overloaded with too much information, and with his once stable boundaries now fuzzy, he fell apart.

The teacher sat at a table with him, setting out trays for sorting red and blue chips. Joel picked up a chip and put it in his mouth.

"No, sweetheart, don't put it in your mouth," the teacher said in a syrupy voice as she took the chip from him. "Put the red chips in this tray, and the blue chips in this tray."

Ignoring her, Joel put another chip in his mouth. This time the teacher responded angrily.

"I said no! No chips in mouth! If you put the chip in your mouth again you'll have to sit in time-out!"

Now in control of the situation, Joel scattered the chips all over the tabletop. The teacher, rather than following through on the time-out threat, positioned herself behind him, forced him to pick up the chips, and then forced him to place them in the correct container.

It made me sick to see her force Joel through the activity, holding his writhing body and making him complete the work, hand-over-hand. It broke my heart as I watched similar situations throughout the day, and Joel responded by throwing one tantrum after another, flinging himself on the floor, kicking and screaming. Never knowing exactly what was expected of him, or how he would be disciplined if he did misbehave, Joel released a host of inappropriate behaviors.

We felt the situation was serious enough to go directly to the teacher's supervisor, Ann Hart. As I handed my notes to her, I felt my pulse beating rhythmically in my ears. Wally and I sat next to each other, holding hands. She read through the notes as we waited.

"I can understand your concern," Ann said. "I've spent some time in the classroom over the past two weeks observing Joel, and I agree with you that he is not likely to learn much in the present atmosphere. I think Joel has a very immature nervous system and needs a calm, disciplined learning environment. I think consistency is the key to Joel's success."

Tears filled my eyes, spilling over. I opened my purse and groped for a tissue. I hated crying in public almost as much as I hated confrontation. My relief, though, was so absolute—I had come expecting a fight, and received instead confirmation that my son's needs were not being met. Instead of excuses, Ann gave the gift of her perception.

Wally broke the silence, not as easily convinced.

"I'm glad you agree there's a problem, but I want you to know we'll pull Joel out of school and keep him at home before we'll send him back under these circumstances. Now, what are you going to do about the problem?"

Ann promised that she would spend as much time as possible over the next few weeks in Joel's classroom, training the teacher and aide. We were welcome to come in at any time.

A one month deadline was set for major changes to be made.

Two weeks later, Ann called. She told me Joel's teacher had left, and a new teacher would be hired within the next few weeks.

We gained an important victory through this time of turmoil. We had fought a battle and won. We had made it clear we would not tolerate an inappropriate classroom setting for Joel. We had learned how to be successful advocates for our son.

Another victory had been won. A victory over the enemies of despair and helplessness. A victory in holding onto the hope that a good education would help Joel grow immeasurably. A victory in not giving in to the "system." A victory in remembering to be constant in prayer.

But with the victory came a sobering thought. This was only the beginning of Joel's school career. Countless educational skirmishes lay ahead of us as we sought what was best for our son. And I was not naive enough to believe all would end on such a positive note.

Lord, I know the battles that lie ahead of us in Joel's education. Each new year holds the possibility of a new room, a new teacher, a new building. With each change comes new problems, new challenges, new accomplishments. Help us, Lord, to hold onto hope, to be patient in times of trouble, and to be constant in our prayers. Amen.

Guilt— The Enemy

Hear my cry, O God;
    listen to my prayer.
From the end of the earth
I call to you,
    when my heart is faint.
Lead me to the rock
    that is higher than I;
for you are my refuge,
a strong tower against
the enemy.

—Ps. 61:1–3

"It's really a very simple choice, Mrs. Bolduc," the doctor said. "You can leave the baby there at the hospital, where they'll put him under the bilirubin lights, or you can take him home. If you choose to take him home, you'll have to bring him in daily for blood tests so we can monitor the bilirubin count. No breast-feeding until we get the jaundice under control."

I've replayed the tape of that conversation several hundred times over the years. It always comes back to five words. "It's your choice, Mrs. Bolduc."

Standing in a noisy hospital waiting room, shaking with fear and holding a brand new baby who resembled a pumpkin, I made a choice. Alone.

I chose to take my son home with me.

Had I chosen differently, Joel might be a typical, precocious twelve-year-old today.

Try living with that.

The guilt reached a boiling point when I found out, four years later, that high bilirubin counts can cause brain damage. None of the doctors we consulted could say for certain if jaundice was the cause of Joel's mental retardation. None of them would rule it out, either.

Guilt creates a black hole in the life of the person who allows it free rein. Guilt saps energy from even the smallest daily tasks. It eats away at relationships, leaving them barren of joy. Living with guilt is like living with a monster that sucks your life force dry, then licks its lips and comes back for more. I know. Guilt was an uninvited guest in my life for five years.

It took over a year of counseling to break through the ravages of that guilt. A year of counseling, as well as the power of the Holy Spirit. Between the two, I learned several lessons.

We do the best we can, with the information we have, at the time we have that information.

We're human beings, not God. We are not omniscient. We are not perfect. We make mistakes.

We stumble and fall often, and it's only by the grace of God that we're able to pick ourselves up again.

We're only able to forgive ourselves if we first open ourselves to God's forgiveness.

Letting go of self-blame is hard. It's like taking a security blanket away from a thumb-sucking toddler. Without that security blanket, life is full of scary things. If it's not my fault, whose fault is it?

The final lesson was the hardest to learn, but the easiest to live with: Accepting God's forgiveness is incredibly freeing.

There are times, even now, on the edge of acceptance, that I slip back into a self-blaming mode. I visualize myself turning back time, standing once again in that hospital room with its overwhelming smell of antiseptic. I talk to the doctor on the phone, ignoring his impatience. I ask more questions. I calm my fears of separation from my baby. I leave my son at the hospital where they put him under the bilirubin lights.

Would this have changed the course of Joel's life? Of my life? I truly don't know. It's a crazy game. A self-defeating game—playing God.

When I'm finished with the game, I center down in prayer, coming before the Lord. I ask for the grace of His forgiveness for falling into the guilt trap once more. Then I get up and get on with my day. One step closer to acceptance.

It's a long, slow walk.

Dear Lord, be my refuge, my rock, my tower of escape from the grasp of guilt. Provide me footholds as I scrabble upward from the pits of self-incrimination. Hear my prayer, Lord. Oh, hear my prayer. Amen.

Talk
to Me!

Sons are indeed a heritage from the LORD, the fruit of the womb a reward.

—Ps. 127:3

I soak up tranquil moments like a thirsty sponge. Family vacations don't afford many such quiet moments, so when Matt asked if he could take the rowboat out for a short ride, I sleepily murmured, "Sure. Don't be long. It'll be dark soon."

Sitting at the end of the pier, eyes closed, I savored the sound of crickets and a cool evening breeze. We were vacationing at a small lake in Michigan. Joel was in bed for the night; Justin was fishing from the pier, and Wally napped on a lounge chair.

"Mom!" Justin's insistent call interrupted my daydream.

"Mom! Look at Matt! He's rowing across the lake!" Justin barely contained his glee. His big brother was sure to get in trouble.

I called out, but the breeze blew my voice back, weak and

powerless. Matt continued to row in long, smooth, powerful strokes toward the opposite shore. I was awestruck by his strength and endurance. He rowed the boat with the intensity of a man, and he was only fourteen.

"Don't worry," I said to Justin. "He'll be right back. There's no light on the boat. He knows enough to come in before dark." I went into the cabin to check on Joel.

When I returned to the pier fifteen minutes later, Justin informed me that Matt hadn't returned yet. I roused Wally from his nap, and together we peered into the distance across the lake. The rowboat was just a speck toward the far shore. Dusk covered the lake like a gloomy gray coverlet. Only the clouds reflected the setting sun. Tinged with red, they glowed in the deepening darkness.

"What can happen?" Wally asked. "He swims well; he's strong enough to row all night, and there's nobody else out there. He'll be back soon."

I sat and fretted in silence. Matt. Strong, silent Matt. There was such distance between us. The little boy who once told me he loved me more than his heart could beat in a million hours no longer talked to me. I felt left out, abandoned. The majority of his time was spent in his room, listening to the stereo and doing homework, or out with friends. When in a sociable mood, it was his dad's company he sought, not mine. I wanted so desperately to talk with him, but he resisted my questions as a scotch-guarded carpet resisted spills. His standard response to my conversational attempts? "Aw, Mom. Leave me alone!"

"Maybe the Loch Ness Monster ate him!" Justin said with a grin. Wally laughed, but I ignored the comment as I moodily crushed a Pepsi can. I thought back over the past few years, and all the times, engrossed in Joel's problems, I had let Matt go his own way. Self-sufficient, self-motivated, self-contained Matt. Busy with his friends and projects, he had always hummed along on his own power, not needing or asking for much attention, seemingly content.

Now I wondered. Did he ask for so little, knowing how little I had left to give? Was it a conscious decision, this self-sufficiency, or had he secretly felt cheated and left out? This disappearance—was it a statement? A plea for attention? Or was it just the action of a normal fourteen-year-old, too involved in his own thoughts and dreams to realize how his actions affected others?

Total darkness. I insisted Wally go to a neighboring cabin and ask for help. We needed a motorboat with a light to search the lake. A fellow, two cabins down, agreed. He and Wally began a slow circuit around the lake.

On shore, my imagination ran rampant. Reel after reel of terrible thoughts crossed my mind like a silent horror film. Drowning. Abduction. Murder.

In desperation, I thought back to Matt's conception. God whispering in the moonlight that something marvelous was happening within my womb. Nine months later, when the doctor laid my firstborn son on my chest, I gazed down on him in wonder. To my astonishment, he met my gaze steadily, eyes wide open, full of wisdom. A moment carved out of eternity.

I took a deep, ragged breath, trying to calm myself. Even Justin showed signs of waning confidence. He put an arm around my shoulder and whispered.

"It'll be all right, Mom. Matt's OK. He's just kind of dumb."

I laughed and squeezed his hand. We prayed out loud together for a few moments. Looking up, we saw the neighbor's boat directly across the lake, still moving slowly. They evidently hadn't found him yet.

Oh God, I cried silently. *Bring my son home!* Two long hours had passed, and a feeling of helplessness crushed my chest, making it hard to breathe.

I remembered all the other prayers I'd said for Matt. I thought back to all the times I had shrugged him off, too tired to talk. All the times I had been too depressed to care, too angry to be kind, too caught up in my worry and fear about Joel to be the mother he needed. I could hardly blame him for building walls. After all, I had stacked the bricks, one by one, with every little rejection. He simply supplied the mortar.

Fourteen. An age for sorting things out, discovering who you are, and where you're headed in life. Matt looked so confident as he walked out into the world each morning, backpack slung over his shoulder. As I scratched his back at night, I realized I hardly knew the person he was becoming. That hurt.

And now he was gone. *Oh God*, I asked, *where is he? Give me another chance. Another chance to share hopes and dreams. Another chance to build bridges, appreciate one another's strengths, forgive one another's weaknesses.*

We heard the hum of the motorboat as it approached our pier. No rowboat in tow. My legs wobbled. I sat down abruptly.

Justin's voice cut the silence. "Look Mom!" He pointed toward the middle of the lake where a gray shape was taking form. A rowboat headed steadily toward us. Matt.

"Where have you been?" Wally yelled. "It's been dark for two hours!" Matt silently moored the boat and hopped up on the dock. I grabbed him in a bear hug, then held him back so I could look at him. He grinned foolishly.

"What's the big deal? What were you doing out in that boat, Dad? I just went for a little ride. It's nice out there in the middle. Real quiet and peaceful. I sat out there for a while, and then I had trouble rowing back. The wind was against me."

Oh, Matt. How I worry and fret and fume, sometimes over nothing. There you sat, content in your boat, enjoying the silence as I envisioned you lost forever. Is this true of our relationship too? All this guilt, all this worry about whether I neglected you in raising Joel. Am I way off track? This distance between you and me—is it natural for your type of personality, for your age, for a firstborn?

Talk to me, Matt. Talk to me!

Lord, I thank you for my firstborn son. I lay my burden of guilt at your feet. Please take it. And help Matt learn to talk to his mother. Amen.

And a Little Child Shall Lead Them

And not only that, but we also boast in our sufferings, knowing that suffering produces endurance, and endurance produces character, and character produces hope, and hope does not disappoint us, because God's love has been poured into our hearts through the Holy Spirit that has been given to us.

—Rom. 5:3–5

Bedtime tuck-ins. Once upon a time they beckoned at the end of my busy days and frantic evenings. A peaceful oasis peopled by the likes of Curious George, the Cat in the Hat, and Wild Things. Prayers and songs, hugs and kisses were spirit restorers. Bad days got better at bedtime. Bath-warmed boys, worn blankies, and favorite stories were miracle workers.

Suddenly I found myself too exhausted to enjoy even this.

I hurried through back scratches and massacred hymns by singing too fast. I no longer read out loud to Matt and Justin. They read enough in school, I rationalized. My nightly routine was to put Joel to bed and retire to my room with a book. Downstairs, Matt and Justin watched TV with their dad. Sometimes they called me in for a quick hug and kiss when they came up to bed. "Let's get this over with" was my theme. I was so tired. So exceedingly tired.

One night, Justin wanted to talk. I made myself comfortable and absentmindedly scratched his back while he prattled on about soccer, and who did what at practice that night.

"Jason's little brother was there tonight."

"Oh?"

"Yeah. Sometimes I wish Joel wasn't handicapped. Especially when I see kids like Jason's brother. He's the same age as Joel, but he's so much fun. He talks a lot, and he's real funny. And he's pretty good at kicking the ball, too."

"I'm sure it's hard, at times, having a brother like Joel."

This turn of the conversation yanked me fully into focus. I made circles with my fingertips, up and down Justin's spine. His voice, muffled by the pillow, was hard to hear. I leaned forward to listen.

"Yeah. I get tired of chasing him around and picking him up when he throws tantrums. He never does what I want him to do. He can be a real pain in the neck."

I murmured in agreement and massaged his shoulders. It suddenly struck me that they were no longer the skinny chicken-wing shoulders of a little boy. My eleven-year-old was growing up. Growing closer to manhood each day. *He suffers too*, I thought. *Lord, he suffers too.*

"But you know what? I was thinking the other day. I'm glad God gave Joel to us. You know why?" He rolled over on his back and looked up at me, his face serious in the shadows.

"Why, honey?"

"Because God knew we would love Joel anyway. He knew we'd take good care of him and teach him as much as we could. If God gave Joel to someone else, they might not have been able to handle him, you know? It takes an awful lot of patience to live with Joel, doesn't it, Mom? I think God knew we would have the patience to love him. So we're lucky, in a way. You know what I mean?"

Oh, my precious son.

"You're absolutely right, Jus. God knew. God knew we would have the patience to love Joel the way he is. And God knew what a super brother you would be. Joel's lucky to have you for a big brother."

I received a sleepy smile in reply. "Thanks, Mom. I love you."

"I love you too, Justin."

Bedtime tuck-ins. Spirit restorers. A time for miracles.

Dear Lord, I come before you in awe of your mysterious ways. I thought I knew all about suffering and endurance. I've been enduring all right. By gritting my teeth. By sheer willpower. By escaping to my room at night. I'd overlooked the rest of the Scripture, Lord. The part about endurance producing character. While my eyes were closed you were building character in the life of my middle son. Character through suffering. And this character building was producing hope. Hope that he, a mere eleven-year-old, then passed on to me.

Oh, Lord! Your Word says that a little child shall lead them. Thank you for making this so in my life. And for opening my eyes and ears to my son's wisdom. Amen.

Running Strong

Be subject to one another out of reverence for Christ. Wives, be subject to your husbands as you are to the Lord. ... Husbands, love your wives, just as Christ loved the church and gave himself up for her. ... Children, obey your parents in the Lord, for this is right. ... Fathers, do not provoke your children to anger, but bring them up in the discipline and instruction of the Lord.

—Eph. 5:21–22, 25; 6:1, 4

Questions bounced between front and back seats as we drove to our first family counseling session.

"How much does this cost, Mom?"

"Eighty-five dollars an hour."

"You're kidding! What a waste! I could buy a pair of Nike Air Jordans for that."

"I think this is more important than shoes, Justin."

"I don't understand why we have to waste money on a dumb shrink. Why don't we use the money and eat at a fancy restaurant once a week?"

"He's not a shrink, Matt. He's a family counselor."

"I don't care. I think it's stupid."

Laughter erupted from the back seat as Matt and Justin

poked and jabbed each other. Wally and I stared at the road ahead, preoccupied with private thoughts as the car carried us to our new counselor. We all suffered an acute case of butterflies.

Like rusted gears in a once efficient piece of machinery, the engine of our family needed oiling. Joel's diagnosis had removed blinders from our eyes and earplugs from our ears. Suddenly, we saw the rust coating our family relationships. We heard the clunks and clanks of a motor in need of oil. We hoped counseling would help our family run smoothly again.

Dr. Downey's down-home manner and easy grin put everyone at ease.

"What do you guys want to talk about?" he asked Matt and Justin.

"I don't even know why we're here," Justin answered in his usual forthright way.

"Sounds like communication would be a good place to start," the doctor said with a laugh. "Thanks for being so honest, Justin."

Communication. Here we go again, I thought. Would the work never end?

By the second session, my internal grumblings had ceased. Communication may be hard work, but the fruit it yields is well worth the labor.

For the first time I shared with Matt and Justin that Joel's constant need for attention wore me out physically and mentally. We brainstormed, looking for solutions. Justin came up with the winning idea.

"I've got it! I'll play with Joel for half an hour every day. When I'm done, Matt can play with him. That gives you an hour to relax, Mom."

One drop of oil, and the motor ran more smoothly.

Wally and I unbottled our frustration at not having enough time for Matt and Justin. We brainstormed again, everyone contributing ideas.

"The problem is trying to do everything together as a family," I said. "Maybe we could split up more often. I'll take

Joel to the zoo, and you take Matt and Justin hiking. Or I'll take one of the boys out for dinner while you and Joel feed the ducks at the park."

This drop of oil really worked. Joel chased ducks, fed penguins, explored the zoo, and had Mom or Dad all to himself once a week. Matt and Justin enjoyed the mall, sports events, or dinner out without a pesky little brother along. Wally and I took pleasure in our boys and rid ourselves of the "guilties" at the same time.

Not all the sessions were so pleasantly helpful.

"I'm tired of the way you treat Joel like royalty." Matt's words hit like a thunderbolt one rainy afternoon. The office exploded with four voices.

Matt had struck a nerve, painful because he spoke the truth. Joel did receive special treatment. We tiptoed around him and went to great lengths in pleasing him. We avoided tantrums at all costs. Matt and Justin were not allowed to get angry with him. The absurdity of a six-year-old calling all the shots leaped out, catching us off guard.

We began treating Joel like "one of the guys." We assigned him chores, just like his brothers. Matt and Justin were responsible for cleaning their bathroom, straightening their bedrooms, and mopping the kitchen floor once a week. Joel's job was to pick up toys before bedtime and help clear the table after dinner. As a result, Matt and Justin liked their little brother much more. They even came to his defense occasionally.

A few more drops of oil, and the clanking settled into a hum.

An amazing thing happened as we exposed our darker thoughts to the sunlight of our late afternoon sessions. Guilt and fear, long hidden, lost their grasp. We discovered that we all felt frustrated, enraged, depressed, and sorry for ourselves at times. That was okay. Even normal. Powerful medicine for eleven- and fourteen-year-old boys. For me and Wally, too.

The equivalent of a whole quart of oil came with the realization that our family was more important than fancy shoes, designer clothes, or expensive dinners out. Our family counted.

By the end of ten sessions, we affirmed Joel as a precious piece of the puzzle making up the Bolduc clan. No one could imagine life without this crazy, zany, often exasperating clown. The five of us fit perfectly together, just as God intended.

Our motor oiled and running strong, we drove straight ahead into the future.

Lord, the words to a hymn keep running through my mind: "There is a balm in Gilead to make the wounded whole. There is a balm in Gilead to heal the sin-sick soul. Sometimes I feel discouraged, and think my work's in vain, but then the Holy Spirit revives my soul again." Thank you for that healing balm, Lord. Amen.

The Essence of Joel

For it was you who
formed my inward parts;
    you knit me together in
    my mother's womb . . .
My frame was not
    hidden from you,
when I was being made
in secret,
    intricately woven in
    the depths of the earth.
Your eyes beheld my
unformed substance.
In your book were written
    all the days that were
    formed for me,
when none of them as yet
existed.

—Ps. 139:13, 15–16

"How's Joel?" The question came at an annual Christmas party from someone I hadn't seen since the last one.

I struggled to say in a few words all we'd been through in the intervening year.

"Joel's—Joel!" It was all I could manage without diving into an hour-long conversation.

How do I put the essence of Joel into words?

His activities—physical therapy, occupational therapy, and speech therapy—define Joel by his deficiencies rather than his strengths. His progress in school, while exciting to me, would not thrill the average parent. While most first-graders are reading and writing at age six, mine is learning to draw horizontal and vertical lines, match the letters of his name, and get through a day without pulling his classmates' hair.

The truly unique side of Joel shines through in his comic nature. His latest joke, in a long line of nonsensical jokes, is "the chicken fell off the waterfall and bumped his head." Where did this joke come from? The same place as "the turkey on the flying trapeze," or "duck on the head!"

Joel is joy in the morning. If a fifty-pound projectile exploding on your soundly sleeping body brings you joy, Joel will make you ecstatic. He doesn't climb out of bed in the morning. He blasts out—a wormy, squirmy missile aimed straight at Mommy's and Daddy's bed.

He pries open sleep-encrusted eyes with insistent fingers. Lifts pajamas looking for a piece of bare belly on which to blow. If all else fails, he sits on the nearest head. Usually mine.

I used to sleep until the last possible moment. Now I force myself out of bed in the darkness of dawn to greet the day and Joel on my own terms. Awake, with coffee bubbling through my bloodstream.

How do I put the essence of Joel into words?

A lean, mean, eating machine who puts away more food than his big brothers combined. And who, in the process, decorates his face, the table, his chair, the floor under his chair, and the person sitting next to him. We considered getting a babysitter for Joel when we take Matt and Justin out to eat. Instead, as a peace offering, we tip our waitresses bountifully.

Joel is perpetual motion. Like the toys in the Duracell commercial, he never wears down. He is plugged into a never-ending power source that, if discovered and channeled, could be marketed for millions.

"Hands Bolduc" is one of Joel's many nicknames. Since infancy he has been obsessed with touching everything within reach. This includes the rear ends of women in front of us in checkout lines, heads of eighty-year-old women sitting behind us in restaurant booths, and bare toes of strangers basking on the beach. "Hands" has caused us many embarrassing moments.

Walls smeared with the contents of diapers, overflowing bathtubs, and toilets clogged with toys are only the tip of the iceberg in Joel's extensive repertoire of shenanigans.

An avid Lawrence Welk fan, Joel especially loves the tap dancing sequences. He nicknamed himself "Tappy Shoes," and loves performing for willing spectators. Feet shuffling, arms flailing, eyes dancing, he is beauty in motion. A music lover at heart, he marches to the beat of his own drum. His rendition of "America," sung in loud falsetto, is capable of causing nerve damage.

How do I put the essence of Joel into words?

For years I prayed for Joel to talk. He was five before he could string together a three-word sentence. My prayers were answered. Now he never stops talking. The problem is he often repeats the same phrase over and over again, sounding like a broken record. This is called perseveration.

Most of these phrases center around water. Joel is obsessed with water. Water fountains, sinks, hoses, creeks, swimming pools, puddles, ponds, toilets, bathtubs, the list goes on. His current oft-repeated sentence is "I wanna go out in the hot tub." He can repeat it up to a hundred times in a ten-minute time span.

I asked Joel's teacher what to do about this perseveration problem.

"Ignore him," she answered.

"Impossible!" I cried.

There is no ignoring Joel. Blue-eyed, blonde and beautiful. Joke teller. First-rate alarm clock. Tap dancer supreme. Master of the massacred hymn. Spotlight seeker. Mischief maker. Water-loving perseverator. Joy bearer.

How's Joel?

Joel's—Joel! Unique. One of a kind. Gift of God.

How in all your creative genius did you ever come up with Joel, Lord? So often his actions cause me pain and frustration. But then he turns around and lights my world with laughter and joy. Thank you for this precious gift. Amen.

The Gift
of Friendship

This is my commandment, that you love one another as I have loved you. No one has greater love than this, to lay down one's life for one's friends.

—John 15:12–13

Jeff's lanky frame lay stretched on its side. Elbow bent and head propped on hand, he helped Joel fit puzzle pieces together. A low buzz of voices filled the Sunday school room as children enjoyed free time. Play dough, crayons, and construction paper made a bright patchwork rug of color across the floor.

Two teenage girls walked down the hall outside the room, peering in as they passed. Stopping abruptly, they pointed at Jeff and giggled. They stood, waiting for him to look up. Evidently, they knew one another. With one lazy wave Jeff both acknowledged and dismissed the girls. He handed Joel another puzzle piece. Having lost Jeff's attention, the girls continued down the hall.

Ten years of experience with high school students told me this was a very special young man. The average seventeen-year-old would have blushed crimson, turned his back, or left Joel to talk with the girls.

Jeff was Joel's special buddy at church.

My initial feeling that this new church was right for us had proved true. On hearing Joel's story, the Christian education director helped us formulate a plan. Paired with a special helper, Joel would mainstream with the four- and five-year-olds. This volunteer would assist Joel with projects beyond his capability and help with behavior management.

Jeff volunteered for the job. A high school senior, he planned to major in occupational therapy in college. He hoped working one-on-one with a child with special needs would confirm the wisdom of his decision.

My pleasure with the arrangement turned to astonishment as I watched the friendship between Jeff and Joel blossom. Joel idolized his new buddy. He greeted Jeff weekly with a kiss on the hand or a hug. Hand in hand they would head for the puzzle corner, pull one out, and sit on the floor. Silly songs, sillier jokes, and laughter filled their time together. At circle time, Jeff helped Joel calm himself enough to listen. When Joel's hands got out of control, Jeff instructed him to hug instead of pulling and grabbing.

It is moving to watch individuals who have a deep love for children with disabilities. Relaxed and accepting, they expect the best from their disabled friends, and usually get it. A loving firmness draws invisible boundaries, keeping behaviors in check. Genuine affection allows plenty of hugs and kisses, so necessary for kids with special needs.

Looking past the disability to the person underneath, these people have a gift for pulling out qualities other people miss. Uncertain and ill at ease around "handicaps," many people ignore the disability completely, make a big deal out of it, respond with false sweetness, or turn away. Often acutely perceptive, the child picks up these clues and escalates behavior accordingly.

We've been blessed with several friends who look past Joel's behavioral problems to the sweet, funny child within.

Wendy, a camp counselor, worked with Joel two summers in a row. Every day she greeted me after camp with a smile and an affirming word about my son. Even on the days he was absolutely rotten, she liked being with him and let me know that. What a gift!

Sarah, a volunteer at the same camp, became one of our most reliable baby-sitters. Intimidated by Joel, most teenagers turned down baby-sitting requests. Sarah viewed baby-sitting for Joel as a privilege. She adored him. Thought he was the cutest kid around. Loved spending time with him.

I'll never forget Joel's seventh birthday. Grandma was there, as well as Aunt Julie, Uncle Gary, and Uncle Dan. Joel greeted all with a big grin and a wriggly hug. They are four of his favorite people.

When the doorbell rang, I sent Joel to answer it, knowing who the special guest would be. Joel opened the door, saw his buddy Jeff, and shrieked. "Jeff!" He ran into the kitchen, leaving Jeff on the doorstep. "Jeff! Jeff!" he screamed. Running back to the door he grabbed Jeff's hand and dragged him into the kitchen. "Jeff!" he announced proudly.

Jeff sat next to Joel during dinner. Hands messy with lasagna, Joel kept reaching for his friend. Jeff didn't mind. He laughed and told Joel to finish his dinner. Dinner completed and hands wiped, Joel took Jeff's hand into his own. He brought it up to his cheek. Smiling with delight, he whispered his friend's name, "Jeff."

The gift of friendship is the best birthday gift of all.

Dear Lord, I thank you for the special friends that grace the lives of each member of this family. I especially thank you for those who have touched Joel's life, lifting up the exterior layers of disability and revealing the beautiful spirit within. Bless them richly, Lord, for these gifts of friendship, so freely given. Amen.

I Will Give You Rest

Come to me, all you that are weary and are carrying heavy burdens, and I will give you rest. Take my yoke upon you, and learn from me; for I am gentle and humble in heart, and you will find rest for your souls. For my yoke is easy, and my burden is light.

—Matt. 11:28–30

It was 8:55 A.M. I'd been up since 6:30, making lunches, doling out bagels and glasses of juice, giving hugs. My prayer time had lasted all of five minutes. Joel, waking earlier than usual, squirmed his way onto my lap with a loud, "Morning, Mom!"

Finally everyone was off to school. I had seven hours to accomplish a myriad of tasks. Laundry. Ironing. Grocery shopping. Shopping for a foster daughter who was moving back in. Lunch with my new pastor's wife, who also has a child with special needs. Writing time. A 2 P.M. meeting with another friend with a special-needs child. To top it all off, I had to cook a decent dinner. We'd eaten takeout three nights in a row.

It's impossible, Lord. Impossible. I poured another cup of coffee and stared out the French doors at the beautiful oranges and reds of autumn. The sight did nothing to lift my gloom. Just the thought of what I wanted to do built pressure in my chest. I walked aimlessly around the kitchen.

Leaving the dishes, I sat in my quiet-time spot and picked up the Bible. *Help, Lord! I can't do all this!* I remembered the still, small voice that had whispered to me in church several weeks earlier. I had written down the words and stuck them in the pages of my Bible. Finding it, I read: "Come before me in the morning with your anxieties. Write them down, one by one, and hand them to me. I will take them willingly. The world's ways are not my ways, child. I offer you new life, a life free of worry and anxiety. Put your trust in me."

I picked up a pen and paper and began listing. I was surprised to find that it was not only that day's chores that overwhelmed me. I was worried about Justin, too. He was struggling in school, and we had requested testing to determine if he had a learning disability. Unhappy with Joel's school placement, we were meeting later in the week with the special education director. It would be a crucial meeting. Crucial to Joel's progress and self-esteem. It truly was too much to handle.

I looked over what I'd written and closing my eyes, I pictured myself handing it to the Lord. God gave me a Scripture.

"Come to me, all who labor and are heavy laden, and I will give you rest." The passage spoke eloquently to this weary, burdened mother.

Yes, the Lord knew exactly how I felt. I was overwhelmed by grief, by burdens too heavy to bear alone. One woman cannot do all and be all for those she loves.

I looked out the living room window. The sun played hide-and-seek through gray clouds, illuminating a single red maple across the street. Burden lifting, my spirit soared.

One thing, Lord. I'll begin with just one thing. And we'll go from there. Together. Amen.

Time Away

But those who wait
for the LORD
   shall renew their
   strength,
they shall mount up
with wings like eagles,
they shall run and
not be weary,
   they shall walk and
   not faint.

—Isa. 40:31

In celebration of our nineteenth wedding anniversary, my husband and I arranged a week away. Just the two of us.

Once or twice a year, we manage a weekend. Every four or five years we somehow stretch it into a week. We take this time away very seriously. We see it as a necessity, not an option.

Reactions from friends vary. Some are delighted for us. These tend to be the friends whose children are grown and gone. Some profess jealousy. Generally, these are the friends with four or five kids, not much money, and no extended family nearby to help with child care. Some are shocked, even disapproving. Unfortunately, many of these are friends with special-needs children. The very friends who need this time away, this respite, the most.

Wendy, Joel's summer camp counselor, agreed to baby-sit the week of our anniversary. Before she could change her mind, we packed our bathing suits and beach paraphernalia, jumped in the car, and headed for Florida.

Without the distraction of the boys, Wally and I had all the time in the world to sit on the beach, doing absolutely nothing. The constant, quiet thunder of the waves washed away tension and worry. I spent hours watching schools of mullet roll in the waves, bellies flashing silver in the sun. Senses heightened, I savored the cool breeze on my sun-warmed back, the smells of salt and fish and suntan oil and sweat, the sugar-fine feel of sand beneath my feet.

Pelicans dive-bombed the water, made a great splash, and came up gulping. A blue heron slowly walked toward the water, each footstep a study in grace. A tiny ghost crab scrabbled in front of my toes and popped down a hole. Wally sat in a chair and read a novel, something he rarely does at home.

The grace of God unfolded around me like the petals of a flower. Slowly. Gently. Inexorably. I found myself moving from *chronos*, man-made time, into *kairos*, God's time. Outside of time I had no needs to fill. I opened myself to waiting on the Lord. My spirit soared skyward into the blue above the sea.

We'd walked this particular beach almost yearly since our marriage. We honeymooned here. Dragging umbrellas, playpens, and diapers, we brought our babies here. We'd made an annual Easter-break pilgrimage to this quiet oasis and measured the growth of our boys against the size of the dunes and the waves.

Once again, it was just the two of us. Nineteen years older (Could it be possible?). Nineteen years wiser. What lessons we'd learned over the preceding fourteen years as parents, and the last six years as parents of a child with special needs.

We desperately needed this time away. Time to rediscover each other. Time to refresh, renew, and rebuild. Time to put things in perspective. Time to wait on God.

Yes, I suppose this can happen at home. Even amid banging doors, ringing telephones, screaming children, beckoning schedules.

But finding time away together, it happens more fully. Together, we experience the quiet grace of God. Together, we renew our strength and mount up with wings like eagles. Together, we return home, changed once more. Made just a tiny bit more into the image of God.

What a blessing. What a promise. What an affirmation of life.

Lord, give me the courage to do whatever it takes to find this time away. Help us find the child care. The money. The strength to make it all work. It's hard, Lord, leaving this child with all of his needs in the care of others. Let me hold onto your promise, Lord. I need so to rise above this weariness. Give me the wings of an eagle to meet the struggles of my daily life. Amen.

Rivers in the Desert

Do not remember
the former things,
or consider the things
of old.
I am about to do
a new thing;
   now it springs
   forth, do you not
   perceive it?
I will make a way in the
wilderness
   and rivers
   in the desert . . .
to give drink to my
chosen people,
   the people whom
I formed for myself
so that they might
declare my praise.

   —Isa. 43:18–19, 20, 21

It was only our second meeting, and yet we had reached a depth I didn't think possible among strangers.

Wally and I had tried support groups before. We had found ourselves frustrated by negativity and lack of spiritual focus.

Deciding to try one more time, we put a notice in our church bulletin. "Wanted. Parents of children with special needs. Forming a group to share information, prayer support, and scriptural insights."

We spent the first meeting getting acquainted. A diverse group, our children's disabilities included mental retardation, autism, Down Syndrome, and severe learning disabilities. One common thread held us together. We all yearned for more hope in our lives. Ron, the father of a son with autism, expressed it best.

"I want to go home from these meetings feeling like yes, there is hope. I want to know that other people have been where I am right now, in the pits of despair, yet climbed out the other side, alive, and in one piece."

I knew by the second meeting that this group would work for us. All the members shared their emotions on discovering their child's disability. We talked about the grace of a supportive church community. We discussed the frustration of finding good medical care and the hope held out by different therapies. We passed books and articles around the circle. Most important, we shared prayer requests, which led into a discussion on healing.

What kind of healing do we pray for? Total wholeness? Enough healing to lead an independent, happy life? Or should we just pray "God's will be done?" What is God's will for these kids anyway? Is it ever the Lord's will that our children suffer? What about healing services? Do we take our children to be anointed with oil and prayed over? What if we do and no visible healing occurs? Would that shake our faith?

Like a bird taking flight, questions flew around the room. There is liberation in discovering that others struggle with the same unanswerable questions.

I shared where I was in my effort to sort it all out.

"I try to accept Joel for who he is, where he is, every single day. I praise God for him, disabilities and all. But I never let go of the hope that he will continue to learn. That one day he will read and write and live independently. Daily I visualize the light of Christ filling his brain, healing broken circuits, restoring damaged areas."

The room was silent for a moment. Ron spoke quietly.

"You know, that's how God deals with us as Christians."

"What do you mean?" I didn't get the connection.

"God tells us He loves and accepts us the way we are, warts and all. Yet He wants us to grow and change—to be more like Christ. Isn't it the same thing? We accept our children the way they are. But we want them to grow toward wholeness. We certainly want them to grow up knowing the love of Christ."

We closed the meeting in prayer and left promising to hold one another, and one another's children, tightly in prayer during the coming month.

I believe everyone left that meeting with hope. Hope that, even in the midst of pain, acceptance is achievable. It may be far away, like a mountain range appearing hazy in the distance. But it is real, not an apparition. Reachable. Climbable. Conquerable.

Lord, thank you for making ways in the wilderness, for providing water in the desert. I thank you for leading us to this group of people who, in their sharing, make our way easier; who hold out hope as an offering, as a spring in the desert. Amen.

Simple Gestures

At that time the disciples came to Jesus and asked, "Who is the greatest in the kingdom of heaven?" He called a child, whom he put among them, and said, "Truly I tell you, unless you change and become like children, you will never enter the kingdom of heaven. Whoever becomes humble like this child is the greatest in the kingdom of heaven."

—Matt. 18:1–4

One of my daily prayer practices is to visualize Jesus sitting on the edge of Joel's bed, laying holy hands on my son's head. Together they sing songs, read books, tell jokes. Always, healing occurs.

Centering down in prayer one day, I saw a different picture. Jesus, sitting on the floor, in the middle of Joel's multihandicapped classroom! All the children gathered around. The teachers stood nearby, transfixed. Joel sat next to Jesus, reaching up and touching his hair, caressing his cheek. Taylor hung on one arm, jumping up and down. Teddy stood behind, arms wound tightly around Jesus' neck. Justin, who is not mobile, was cradled on Jesus' lap; and Thomas, who seldom looks anyone in the eye, stared intently into Jesus' face. The room reverberated with Trevor's excited shrieks and Daniel's monotone song.

As this amazing scene unfolded, Joel took Jesus' hand into his own. Such a large hand in the small hand of my son. Joel examined that hand, the hand that fashioned the heavens and the earth, as if it were as common as his father's. Finding a small scratch, he leaned down and kissed it.

"Hurt," Joel said. Tenderly he kissed it again.

"Thank you," Jesus replied seriously. "Feels better already!"

"Hurt," Joel insisted. "Band-Aid."

Jesus looked up at the teacher and nodded. She went to the closet, got the Band-Aids, and handed the box to Jesus. He gave one to Joel.

Fingers fumbling, Joel tried to pull off the wrapper. Lacking the fine motor control needed for the task, he whined in frustration. Jesus helped, patiently guiding Joel's fingers to place the Band-Aid on the scratch.

Such a simple gesture. So childlike, this concern for someone's hurt. It pierced my heart, and with the piercing came new understanding.

Despite his disabilities, maybe even because of them, Joel is a clear channel of God's love. A conduit unblocked by worldly fears, preoccupations, idols, and cares.

I wondered. What would my reaction be, if confronted with the living Christ? Would I stammer and stutter in self-consciousness? Search for words, and find none worthy of his hearing? Slink to the back of the crowd, afraid of embarrassing myself? Probably.

Through this vision, God opened a window in my clouded and imperfect vision of the world. My son, whom I had viewed as broken, greeted the living Christ with a kiss. A kiss to the hand that was nailed to the cross two thousand years ago. A child, a child with mental retardation, ministering to the Lord.

What is brokenness?

What is wholeness?

Surely, in the eyes of his Lord, my son is perfectly whole.

Lord, help me relinquish my fear, my impatience, my yearning for wholeness as the world knows wholeness. Let me see the presence of the kingdom in the simple gestures of everyday life with Joel.

Joy
Rekindled

When a woman is in labor, she has pain, because her hour has come. But when her child is born, she no longer remembers the anguish because of the joy of having brought a human being into the world.

—John 16:21

Joel's eighth birthday shimmers brightly in my memory. Past birthdays had been more traumatic than celebratory as they revealed the unavoidable truth of Joel's disability. Everything he lacked glared accusingly in the light of those birthday candles. At two he could not yet walk. At three he did not have the social skills necessary to play with other children. At four he still wore diapers. At five he spoke in two-word sentences. At six he could not ride a bike. What would the milestone birthday of sixteen bring? Eighteen? Twenty-one?

I prepared for the birthday party with mixed emotions. In the past year Joel had made so much progress, especially in communication skills and the ability to control his behavior. But what might the coming year hold? Would he ever learn to tie his shoes, to eat without making a mess, to read and write?

Walter Wangerin writes, "It is the experience of genuine grief that prepares for joy." This eighth birthday party was living proof of that statement.

Joel opened his presents slowly, savoring each in turn (this, my hyperactive son who had previously whined and cried through Christmas and birthday commotion).

"New shoes! Thank you, Grandma! My teacher's gonna love 'em," his voice rang out, full of delight (this, my son who at six had spoken in two- and three-word sentences).

As his daddy wheeled a new bike into the kitchen, Joel's entire body trembled with excitement; his face glowed with pure pleasure. Jumping on it, he rode circles through the kitchen, study, and hallway (this, my son whom I had once feared would never walk). The kitchen filled with the music of his laughter as well as with ours.

This birthday we *celebrated*! This birthday we knew the true meaning of joy. The bubbling, breathless joy that comes to fill the vacuum created by despair and hopelessness. The joy that overcomes the pain of childbirth. The joy that greets the empty tomb on Easter morning.

Dear Lord, thank you for rekindling our sorrow into joy. May all those who grieve for their children know that you are there, longing to comfort them in their despair; longing to give them the gift of joy. Amen.

The Maestro

Now we have
received not the spirit of
the world, but the Spirit
that is from God, so that
we may understand the
gifts bestowed on us by
God . . . in words not
taught by human
wisdom, but taught by
the Spirit.

—1 Cor. 2:12–13

Wally and I recently met once again with our church's director of Christian education. The subject of our meeting? Joel. We had lost our special buddy, Jeff, to graduation and college six months earlier, and subsequent volunteers had not worked out. Joel's behavior in Sunday school had grown progressively worse. In frustration, we had stopped taking him to Sunday school, taking him with us to the first twenty or thirty minutes of worship instead.

The director was frustrated, too. Joel had thrown a monkey wrench into her well-run Sunday school program.

"We need to know more about Joel," she said. "Tell us about

his diagnosis, his I.Q., his learning style, his behavioral problems." It was evident that she sincerely wanted to help. "Let's attack this problem as a team," she ended with enthusiasm.

We talked for over an hour before it dawned on me. We were discussing a "problem," rather than Joel.

"I wish you really knew Joel," I said passionately. "All you see are the outward manifestations of his disability—the hair pulling, the short attention span, the difficulties in learning. Under all of that is a very precious little boy with strengths as well as weaknesses."

I went home feeling discouraged once again.

When will the church accept Joel (and others like him) for who they are, rather than focus on what they can or cannot do?

When will the church love Joel (and others like him) with a no-strings-attached kind of love?

When will the church wake up and realize that a child with mental retardation (or cerebral palsy, or autism, or blindness, or deafness) may minister to the most wise among us?

I watched Joel minister to a good-sized portion of our congregation not too long ago. We had slipped into worship late, luckily finding an aisle seat near the front of the sanctuary. Everyone had just risen for the first hymn, "A Mighty Fortress Is Our God." Joel craned his neck, intently scrutinizing the faces on either side of us as well as behind us, as he usually does. The organ swelled and the sanctuary resounded with several hundred voices. Joel, music lover extraordinaire, was quickly caught up in the soul of the music.

Attention shifting from the people around us to the choir and choir director, Joel watched a moment before raising an imaginary baton. Becoming one with the music, he conducted the choir magnificently, keeping perfect time.

Attention shifting again, he noticed that an entire section of the congregation stood facing us. Joel stepped out into the aisle, turned toward the sea of faces, assumed his best conductor pose, raised his imaginary baton, and proceeded to lead his own personal "choir" through the last two stanzas of the hymn.

My first reaction was one of embarrassment. Presbyterians

are sometimes jokingly referred to as the "Frozen Chosen," and Joel's Spirit-led behavior was definitely out of the ordinary. My hand itched to reach out and pull him back into the pew, but I held myself back. Glancing around, I was greeted by smiles on all sides.

Joel gave the church a gift that day. The gift of Spirit-led worship.

How I long to stand up and shout:

Please accept my child for who he is.
Love him for his strengths and forgive his weaknesses.
Open your arms in welcome and say, "It's great to see you!"
Open your eyes and see the flame of the Holy Spirit within,
* glowing clear and bright and strong.*

Lord, I've prayed it before and I'll pray it again. Help the church be the church. Amen.

I'm Naked and I'm Dancing!

David danced before the LORD with all his might.

—2 Sam. 6:14

Wally and I sat in the living room, enjoying our coffee in the early morning quiet. Matt and Justin had already left for school; we'd just finished our devotions, and Joel was still asleep. The tranquillity evaporated with the squeak of bedsprings, the loud *thunk* and pitter-patter of feet overhead, followed by the bang of a door.

Joel was up.

Sipping my coffee and quickly scanning the newspaper headlines, I waited, knowing my day was about to begin in earnest. There would be no time for a second cup of coffee or perusing the paper until Joel was safely on the bus.

Suddenly, silence, followed a few moments later by the clanging of the laundry chute. Part of Joel's morning routine is to jump out of bed, undress immediately, and throw his pj's, clean or dirty, down the chute. Silence again, broken this time by Joel's voice, loud and exuberant.

"I'm naked and I'm dancing!"

Wally and I burst into laughter and raced each other to the stairs, Wally shouldering his way in front of me. Sure enough, Joel was naked and dancing with abandon in the upstairs hallway. Feet shuffling and arms flailing, he did his best Fred Astaire imitation, then spun crazily, filling the narrow space of the hallway with a cyclone of praise. His body posture and face reflected pure joy—his wake-up jig a prayer of thanksgiving for the gift of the day. It put my quiet, closed-eye morning prayers to shame. Wally grabbed him in a bear hug, but Joel wriggled free to dance some more.

What an amazing gift we were given that morning—a glimpse into the freedom of spirit that must await us on the other side of life, when we join with the angels in never-ending praise. As I reflect back on it, I am reminded of David dancing mightily, in near nakedness, before the Lord. Body, mind, and spirit given completely in praise and worship. No mask, no pretense, no covering. Simply pure, unadulterated praise.

How many can stand before the Lord in total nakedness? I think of Adam and Eve in the Garden before their eyes were opened by sin. They walked naked, without shame, free from the need to cover up physically or psychologically. Joel's naked dancing suggested what it might be like to walk with the Lord if I were totally comfortable with myself, of what it might be like to worship God with no requests, no petitions, no questions, no shame.

Maybe these are the lessons I am to learn from this child. How to be open and vulnerable. How to live in the moment. How to greet the day with simple joy.

I remember the words of a hymn we sang often in the church we attended when Joel was baptized . . .

> I danced in the morning when the world was begun,
> And I danced in the moon and the stars and the sun,
> And I came down from heaven
>   and I danced on the earth—at Bethlehem I had my birth.
> Dance, then, wherever you may be,

I am the Lord of the Dance, said he,
And I'll lead you all, wherever you may be,
And I'll lead you all in the dance, said he.

Lord, help me learn to dance before you in spiritual nakedness, to give myself to you just as I am. Bless me with a teachable heart, Lord, that I may not miss the daily lessons my children provide. Amen.

The
Sacred Place

Sing aloud to God
our strength;
    shout for joy to the
    God of Jacob. . . .
I hear a voice
I had not known:
"I relieved your shoulder
of the burden;
    your hands were
    freed from the basket.
In distress you called,
and I rescued you;
    I answered you in the
    secret place of thunder."
                    —Ps. 81:1, 5, 6–7

Joel and Wally fill a small sack with apples and trail mix.

"Goin' on a hike!" Joel's face beams his pleasure. He runs and grabs his coat, laying it on the chair as he's been taught. Reaching back he finds an armhole, wiggles his arm in, then shrugs the coat up, and inserts the other arm. He grins at this new accomplishment.

"See you later," he says as he and Wally walk out the back door.

"Have fun!" I call toward their retreating backs. Turning around, Joel blows me a kiss. "Have fun, Mom!" he yells. I stand on the deck and watch them disappear into the 2,500-acre woods behind the house, part of a county park. Taking advantage of the quiet time, I pull up a chair to the umbrella table and let the dinner dishes sit in the sink.

The lonely hoot of an owl carries across the air. Swallows dip and soar in the twilight sky, and finches crowd the bird feeder. How I love living on the edge of this park. It's so peaceful and quiet, especially in the evening. Wildlife abounds—deer, raccoon, Canada geese, rabbits, and birds by the thousand.

The tranquillity lulls me into contemplation. I remember loading Joel into the same worn, yellow backpack that carried both his brothers before him. I see the five of us hiking down the creek for a fossil hunt. I hear the echo of excited voices as they scoop up treasures. How our pockets bulged, clunking heavily, on the hike home. Matt's and Justin's shelves still hold the best of those fossils.

Skimming across the years, my mind lights on another memory—this one tinged with sadness. Joel, a toddler who can't toddle. Two years old and not yet walking. Me, worried and stressed. The two of us home alone during the week. Me, grabbing the backpack, putting it on the table, lifting Joel into it, and hoisting him onto my back. Tromping into the woods, Joel's weight adding to the burden of worry that makes my shoulders ache at night. My head full of churning questions. Why are his muscles so floppy? Will he ever walk? Will he need a wheelchair? In time the peace of the forest seeps down and quiets my mind. The damp coolness softening the air, the melodic song of cardinals, and the crunch of twigs underfoot restores a sense of balance. Only then do the prayers come.

Then came the hardest years. I see myself escaping into the woods and finding a fallen tree trunk to lean against. The sound of the birds as I sit here on the deck reminds me of the birds' song then. How I marveled, even in the midst of panic, at the beauty. Sitting in nature's cathedral of praise, I called out to God in anguish before sinking into silent and wordless meditation.

Looking at the swing set and sandbox recently built for Joel on the woods' edge, those times of despair melt into a later memory. We're in the woods again, exploring its mysteries. Joel plops down and probes the dirt with a stick, searching for worms. I meditate on sunlight streaming through the green canopy of leaves overhead, relish the texture of moss beneath my fingertips, and wonder at the way bark grows differently on each species of tree.

The words of a friend who has a child with Down Syndrome echo through the darkening silence.

"I kept praying for the Lord to change my son," she said. "He changed me instead."

From my vantage point on the deck, overlooking the backyard, the woods, and the past, I know that I too am a changed person. I no longer walk side by side with fear and sadness. Somewhere along the journey courage and joy grabbed my hand and held on tight.

I once looked at Joel and couldn't see past the pain of his disability. When I gaze on him now, I see a myriad of Joels. Joel, the baby of the family. Joel, the clown. Joel, the stubborn. Joel, the giver of love. Joel, the exuberant, the loud, the singer, the dancer. Joel, who will always struggle to learn.

The future still holds many questions. Will Joel ever read? Write? Hold a job? Live independently? How dependent will he be on us in our later years? What part will Matt and Justin play in his life? If I allow it, the uncertainty still has the power to overwhelm and suck me into a trap of worry and fear.

From my vantage point here on the deck, I realize this forest behind our house has been my place of sacred thunder. The place God spoke to me. The place I began to listen. Whenever the questions get too frightening or complex, I know this place awaits. A place of balance and peace and tranquillity. A place to seek the face of God.

Looking up, I see the bright red of Joel's sweatshirt peeking through the green underbrush. His voice mingles with Wally's laughter. I know they too have been touched by this sacred place. Touched by the hand of God.

It won't be long before Joel and Wally will be loading backpacks and camping gear into the trunk of the car. I'll stand in the driveway and wave good-bye as they head for the mountains. Before going into the quietly waiting house, I will say a prayer of thanksgiving. Thanksgiving for the strength and deliverance given us on this journey through life. For the sustenance given us by God. Sustenance as real as apples and trail mix. The Bible calls it manna, bread from heaven.

Lord, it hasn't been an easy journey. You, above all, know that. But I've learned so much in the struggle and the pain. About perseverance and patience and forgiveness. About grief and joy and acceptance. The most important lesson was letting go. Letting go of my preconceptions of my child. Letting go of the world's vision of perfection. Letting go of the myth of self-sufficiency. Thank you, Lord, for all you've taught me along the way. I especially thank you for the gift of Joel. A little child has led us. Amen.

Epilogue

In this you rejoice, even if now for a little while you have had to suffer various trials, so that the genuineness of your faith—being more precious than gold that, though perishable, is tested by fire—may be found to result in praise and glory and honor when Jesus Christ is revealed.

—1 Pet. 1:6–7

One of the amazing outcomes of the healing process is the ability to look back into the pain and see threads of gold glimmering in the darkness. Flashes of insight, like glittering jewels, leave me breathless at times—breathless with awe at the incredible power and goodness of God.

As I ended my morning prayers recently, my vision came to rest on the bookcase Wally built for me one Christmas. This bookcase shelves not only my favorite books but treasured family photographs and mementos as well. There, amid my most precious possessions, are the words to a song titled "The Miracle of Joel." The song was written by a dear friend as a gift for Joel's baptism, handwritten in calligraphy and elaborately framed by another wonderful friend.

I re-read the words as if for the first time:

The Miracle of Joel

So many years ago You came to light the way.
And yet at times I feel You've grown so far away.
I pray to see Your love in a way that keeps me strong.
The world I face each day tells me that You're gone.

Then You give us a miracle of joy.
God touched our lives with a baby boy.
And he's growing in the love of our Lord.

You touched the eyes of men and helped the blind
    to see.

Why must I be blind to what You gave for me?
I struggle every day with a life that seems so wrong.
Our paths grow far apart; I turn and find You gone.

Then You give us a miracle of joy.
God touched our lives with a baby boy.
And he's growing in the love of our Lord.

Two hearts You joined in love and bonded them through
  prayer
The gift You give to them, we dedicate our care.
With each new breath he takes we know You're here to
  stay
The hand of God reached down and touched the world
  today.

Then You give us a miracle of joy.
God touched our lives with a baby boy.
And he's growing in the love of our Lord.

Yes, Joel's growing in the love, growing in the love,
growing in the love of our Lord.

—*Randy G. Darcy*

Illumination! Although I'd read them numerous times before, the words suddenly took on new meaning. No longer were they Randy's words, Randy's testimony, Randy's praise for the miracle of new life. They were my words, my testimony, my hymn of thanksgiving for the miracle of Joel. Only the Holy Spirit could have inspired our friend to write words that would speak to me eight years later of the struggle and the doubt yet to come. Of the spiritual blindness that would afflict me. Of the strengthening bond of prayer as my marriage would threaten to fall apart. Of the awakening that would finally take place in my heart with the realization of the true miracle of Joel—the miracle of a precious little boy, healthy in body, impaired in mind, but totally intact in spirit. A gift from the hand of God, given to our care, to raise in the love of our Lord.

Woven into the dark hues of the tapestry of our family life over the past thirteen years are glittering threads of gold—the preciousness of a faith, tested by fire, that enables me to raise my voice in praise today.

Yes, Joel's growing in the love, growing in the love, growing in the love of our Lord. All praise, honor, and glory are yours, dear Lord. Amen.